NOW YOU KNOW

KNOW

CANADA'S HEROES

NOW YOU KNOW

CANADA'S HEROES

Doug Lennox

DUNDURN PRESS
TORONTO

Editor: Edward Butts
Copy Editor: Allison Hirst
Design: Courtney Horner
Printer: Webcom

Library and Archives Canada Cataloguing in Publication

Lennox, Doug
     Now you know Canada's heroes / by Doug Lennox.

ISBN 978-1-55488-444-5

       1. Heroes--Canada--Biography. 2. Canada--Biography.
I. Title.

FC25.L46 2009   971.009'9   C2009-902994-4

1   2   3   4   5   13   12   11   10   09

Conseil des Arts
du Canada

Canada Council
for the Arts

ONTARIO ARTS COUNCIL
CONSEIL DES ARTS DE L'ONTARIO

We acknowledge the support of The Canada Council for the Arts and the Ontario Arts Council for our publishing program. We also acknowledge the financial support of the Government of Canada through the Book Publishing Industry Development Program and The Association for the Export of Canadian Books, and the Government of Ontario through the Ontario Book Publishers Tax Credit program, and the Ontario Media Development Corporation.

Care has been taken to trace the ownership of copyright material used in this book. The author and the publisher welcome any information enabling them to rectify any references or credits in subsequent editions.

J. Kirk Howard, President

www.dundurn.com

Dundurn Press	Gazelle Book Services Limited	Dundurn Press
3 Church Street, Suite 500	White Cross Mills	2250 Military Road
Toronto, Ontario, Canada	High Town, Lancaster, England	Tonawanda, NY
M5E 1M2	LA1 4XS	U.S.A. 14150

CANADA'S
HEROES

contents

preface

Most Canadians are well aware that our country has many heroes: men, women, and even children who have excelled in various endeavours or shown bravery or resourcefulness in war, disaster, and other trying situations. We learn about some of our heroes in school, people such as Sir Isaac Brock, Laura Secord, Tecumseh, William Lyon Mackenzie, and Louis-Joseph Papineau. Many of our heroes have been athletes who, in both amateur and professional competition, consistently perform far above the average. Canadian heroes are honoured with statues, monuments, and plaques. Their names have been given to rivers, mountains, highways, and public buildings. Their images have appeared on stamps, their life stories have been written by biographers, and some have been the subjects of television documentaries and feature films.

Many of Canada's heroes haven't been soldiers, police officers, renowned explorers, or hockey stars, but ordinary people who found it within themselves to do something extraordinary in a life-or-death situation: a railroad worker who prevented a train wreck after a disastrous land slide, a wounded child who dragged an unconscious parent out of a shattered house following a devastating explosion, a movie projectionist whose quick thinking saved children from a killer fire. And, of course, we have had heroes like Terry Fox who gave themselves unselfishly to a noble cause.

For every Canadian hero whose name is well remembered, there are many more who, over the years, have become obscure. They fought in wars, won medals, charted unknown wilderness, made spectacular scientific discoveries, and helped people in need. At one time they were headline news, but now they are largely forgotten.

This thoroughly researched volume contains hundreds of stories about Canadian heroes. Readers will find fascinating facts about great Canadians they thought they already knew, and learn the thrilling stories of brave Canadians of whom they were previously unfamiliar. Read on, and spend some time with these remarkable heroes of Canada.

courage in battle

What is the Valiants Memorial (*Monument aux Valereux*)?

The Valiants Memorial is a monument in Ottawa, commemorating 14 representative figures from Canada's military history. There are nine busts and five full statues, all life-sized, by artists John McEwen and Marlene Hilton Moore. The work is located around the Sappers Staircase, adjacent to the National War Memorial. On the wall of the staircase is a quotation from the Roman poet Virgil's *The Aeneid* — *Nulla dies umquam memori vos eximet aevo.* (No day will ever erase you from the memory of time). The monument was dedicated on November 5, 2006, by Governor General Michaëlle Jean. The heroes represented in the monument are:

From the French Regime
- Le Comte de Frontenac
- Pierre le Moyne d'Iberville

From the American Revolution
- Thayendanegea (Joseph Brant)
- John Butler

From the War of 1812
- Major General Sir Isaac Brock, KB
- Laura Secord
- Charles de Salaberry

From the First World War
- Georgina Pope
- General Sir Arthur Currie, GCMB, KCB
- Corporal Joseph Kaeble, VC, MM

From the Second World War
- Lieutenant Robert Hampton Gray, VC, DSC
- Captain John Wallace Thomas, CBE
- Major Paul Triquet, VC, CD
- Pilot Officer Andrew Mynarski, VC

Where was Canada's "Thermopylae"?

On the banks of the Ottawa River's Long Sault Rapids, in May of 1660, a band of 17 Frenchmen led by a young adventurer named Adam Dollard, with the assistance of about 40 Native allies, stood off an Iroquois force of hundreds that was en route to attack Montreal. The siege at the Long Sault lasted for a week before the Iroquois finally forced their way into the small stockade and massacred the defenders. However, because of the heavy casualties they had suffered in overpowering Dollard's men, the Iroquois abandoned the plan to attack Montreal. This conflict in the Canadian wilderness has been compared to the ancient Battle of Thermopylae, in which 300 Spartan warriors held off a mighty Persian army for three days.

Quickies

Did you know ...

- that during both world wars, the Canadian government used the story of Adam Dollard's heroism as a recruiting aid to encourage young men to join the armed forces?

Who were Butler's Rangers?

They were a company of Loyalist militia commanded by Colonel John Butler during the Revolutionary War. They operated mostly out of Fort Niagara, usually in the company of Native Allies. Butler's Rangers proved to be a very effective fighting force in the western theatre of the war. After the war the Rangers disbanded and most of the men settled in Upper Canada. Many people today who are of United Empire Loyalist stock proudly trace their ancestry back to members of Butler's Rangers.

Quickies

Did you know ...

- that a little-known hero of the Revolutionary War Battle of Quebec was a riverman named Jean Baptiste Bouchette, known to his colleagues as *La Tourte* (Wild Pigeon)? He smuggled the governor of Quebec, Guy Carleton, who had been in Montreal, past American lines so he could get into Quebec City to take command.

Why are the Loyalists remembered as heroes in Canada?

Some Loyalists, like John Butler and John Graves Simcoe, the founder of Toronto, were war heroes. Most of the Loyalists were farmers, tradesmen, and businessmen who were persecuted in the American colonies during the Revolutionary War and after it because they had refused to join what they believed was a treasonous rebellion. After losing everything they owned in the Revolution and its aftermath, they became the pioneers who established the new British colonies of Upper Canada and New Brunswick.

Who were the Canadian Rangers?

During the Revolutionary War, Captain William Caldwell, an Irish-born British officer, led a Loyalist militia unit that became known as the Canadian Rangers. Operating out of Detroit and Niagara, the Rangers were one of the most effective fighting forces in the western theatre of the war, and Caldwell was among the most daring and successful of commanders. The Rangers and their Native allies struck deep into enemy territory and won major victories at Sandusky (Ohio) and Blue Licks (Kentucky). After the war, Caldwell moved to Upper Canada, but was one of the British agents who encouraged the Natives to fight American expansion. In the War of 1812, the aging Caldwell commanded a ranger force again. At the Battle of Moraviantown, when General Henry Proctor's British troops broke and ran, Captain Caldwell and his Rangers stayed to fight a rearguard action alongside Tecumseh and his warriors. Caldwell died in 1822. In American histories he and his Canadian Rangers are bloodthirsty villains. In Canada they are Loyalist heroes.

Why is Sir Isaac Brock called the Saviour of Upper Canada?

When the United States declared war on Great Britain in June of 1812, its main goal was the seizure of the British colonies of Upper and Lower

Canada. Major General Isaac Brock, the military commander of Upper Canada, had a long frontier to defend with relatively few troops. Morale among the civilian population was low. In fact, the confident Americans had boasted that the conquest of Canada would be "a mere matter of marching." In spite of the seemingly impossible odds against him, Brock stopped a numerically superior American army in its tracks, and gave the people of Upper Canada reason to believe that they actually could defeat the Americans.

What were the circumstances of Brock's death at Queenston Heights?

On the night of October 12–13, a large American force crossed the Niagara River and landed near the village of Queenston. In the morning, when Brock arrived from Fort George, about 7.5 miles away, he found that American soldiers had taken a strategic position atop the heights overlooking Queenston and the river. Without waiting for reinforcements that were on the way, Brock rallied some troops behind him and led a charge uphill toward the American position. His general's uniform made him a tempting target, and he was shot twice; first in the hand, and then through the breast. The Americans were eventually driven back across the river, but Brock's death was a severe blow to the British and Canadians. For the remainder of the war the British would be unable to find another general of his calibre.

What were Brock's dying words?

At least three supposed dying statements have been attributed to Brock. The one most quoted is "Push on, brave York volunteers." He is also alleged to have said, "My fall must not be noticed or impede my brave companions from advancing to victory." If that seems a bit wordy for a dying man, another account has him uttering a single word in Latin, *Surgite*, which could be interpreted as "Press on." Actually, Brock most likely died without saying a word. George Jarvis, a 15-year-old militiaman was just a few feet from Brock when he was shot. He saw Brock fall and later reported, "Running up to him, I enquired, 'Are you much hurt, Sir?' He placed his hand on his breast and made no reply, and slowly sunk down."

How have Canadians honoured Sir Isaac Brock?

On October 16, 1812, Brock was buried at Fort George with full military honours, along with Lieutenant Colonel John Macdonell, who was also killed in the battle. The remains of both soldiers are now in Brock's Monument, a 184-foot tower at Queenston. The city of Brockville, Ontario, was named in his honour. There is a Brock Township in Ontario and a Village of Brock in Saskatchewan. St. Catharines, Ontario, has Brock University. In Ontario, several roads and schools have been named after Brock. In Britain, Isaac Brock was made a Knight of the Bath.

Quickies

Did you know ...

- that Isaac Brock never knew that he had been knighted? On the very day he died, the church bells in London were ringing in celebration of his victory at Detroit. News travelled slowly in 1812.

Why is Laura Secord called the Heroine of Upper Canada?

Legend has it that Laura Secord was a Canadian girl who overheard some drunken American soldiers discussing a planned attack on the small force of Lieutenant James Fitzgibbon, and walked through the woods with a cow so she could bluff her way past American patrols, and warn the lieutenant. Actually, Laura Secord was the American-born wife of a Canadian militiaman, and was 38 years old at the time of her famous walk through the woods. She did not have a cow with her. No one is certain just how she learned of the American attack. There are several versions of the story.

How dangerous was Laura Secord's mission?

It was a very dangerous undertaking. She had to travel on foot about 20 miles through rough country full of wolves and rattlesnakes. If she'd been caught by an American army patrol, she might have been shot as a spy. There were also gangs of men who passed themselves off as militia fighting for the Americans, but who were in fact little more than ruffians and bandits; not the sort of characters a woman travelling alone would have wanted to encounter. By the time Laura reached Lieutenant Fitzgibbon's camp, her shoes were in tatters and her feet were bleeding and blistered. Quite likely Fitzgibbon's Native scouts had already told him of the approaching Americans, but that takes nothing away from Laura Secord's heroic act. The Americans were completely routed at the Battle of Beaver Dams on June 24, 1813.

Who knew of Laura's heroism?

At the time, very few people knew of it. She herself did not boast of it. In 1820, 1827, and 1837, Fitzgibbon wrote letters confirming that she had indeed made the perilous journey. In 1845, her son Charles wrote a letter about it to a Cobourg periodical. In 1853, Laura wrote a narrative for a Toronto publication. But these accounts drew scant attention. Then, in 1860, the Prince of Wales (later King Edward VII) was in Niagara Falls to officiate at a ceremony honouring Sir Isaac Brock. He heard the story of Laura Secord's walk through the woods, and was fascinated by it. He gave the 85-year-old woman an honorarium of 100 pounds in gold. This brought Laura national attention, and she was on her way to becoming a Canadian icon. She died in 1868 at the age of 93.

How did Tecumseh die?

On October 5, 1813, an American army led by General William Henry Harrison attacked a retreating British army commanded by General Henry Proctor near Moraviantown on the Thames River in the southwestern part of Upper Canada. The British troops broke rank and ran, but their Native allies, led by Tecumseh, stayed and fought. Tecumseh was shot and killed. His warriors carried the body off and buried it secretly. Several different Americans, including future vice president Richard Mentor Johnson would claim the "honour" of having shot Tecumseh, but none would be able to satisfactorily prove the claim.

What Canadian officer was once addressed as "Marquis of cannon powder"?

Lieutenant Colonel Charles de Salaberry was the grandson of a soldier who had fought for New France against the British, and the son of a soldier who had fought for the British against the Americans. He himself was a career soldier in the British army. On October 26, 1813, at the Battle of Châteauguay, in spite of being heavily outnumbered, de Salaberry routed an American invasion force that was advancing on Montreal. This victory made de Salaberry a legendary figure in Quebec.

Seven More Canadian Heroes of the War of 1812

- Captain Joseph Barss: commander of the privateer ship *Black Joke*, the scourge of the American coast.
- Lieutenant General Gordon Drummond: won the Battle of Lundy's Lane.
- Dr. William "Tiger" Dunlop: British army surgeon who treated wounded soldiers from both armies, sometimes under horrific conditions.
- William Green: teenaged boy who spied on American camp at Stoney Creek and gave the British/Canadian forces valuable information, including the password for the pickets.
- Lieutenant Colonel John Harvey: won the Battle of Stoney Creek.
- Lieutenant Colonel John W. Morrison: won the Battle of Crysler's Farm.
- John Norton: Mohawk Chief and British ally who fought in several engagements on the Niagara Frontier, including Queenston and Stoney Creek.

Who was the first Canadian soldier to be awarded the Victoria Cross?

On October 25, 1854, at Balaclava during the Crimean War, Lieutenant Alexander Roberts Dunn from York (Toronto) was one of the horsemen in the legendary Charge of the Light Brigade. A mistaken order had sent the Six Hundred into the Valley of Death. When the surviving cavalrymen began to withdraw, Lieutenant Dunn saw three Russians bearing down on a British sergeant whose horse had been wounded. Wielding his sabre, Dunn attacked the Russians and killed all three of them, allowing the sergeant to get back to his own lines. Then Dunn galloped to the rescue of a private who was in peril, and killed a fourth Russian with his sabre. Two years later Dunn was among the first recipients of a new medal awarded by the British Crown for valour in the face of the enemy, the Victoria Cross.

Quickies

Did you know ...

- that between 1854 and 1945, 95 Canadians were awarded the Victoria Cross, the British Empire's highest military decoration? Considering Canada's population over that period, Canadians won more VCs per capita than any other Commonwealth nation. Twenty-eight of the Canadians awarded the VC were killed in action, and another seven died of wounds received in the action for which the VC was awarded. The prestige that came with this medal could hardly be comprehended today. A returned soldier who could put VC after his name was a national hero. In many instances he came home to a grand welcoming committee, a parade, and a banquet. Men who were awarded the medal posthumously had parks, streets, and mountains named after them.

What was the connection between the War of 1812 and a Black Canadian who was awarded a Victoria Cross?

William Edward Hall's father was a captive aboard an American slave ship that was intercepted by a Royal Navy vessel during the War of 1812 and taken to Halifax. His mother was a slave on a plantation near Washington D.C. when the British attacked and burned the city. She escaped and boarded a British ship which took her to Halifax. Their son William enlisted in the Royal Navy and was at Lucknow, India, in 1857 at the time of the Sepoy

Rebellion. Hall was a gunner on HMS *Shannon,* which was part of a naval force trying to breach the walls of an enemy fortification. Grenades and musket fire killed or wounded almost all of the British gunners. Hall and one injured officer, working the only gun that was still operable, and under intense enemy fire, blasted a hole in the wall that enabled British troops to take the position. Hall was awarded the Victoria Cross, making him the first Canadian to win the VC in a naval action. He died in 1904, and the inscription on his gravestone in Avonport, Nova Scotia, says that he was the "first man of colour to win the Empire's highest award for valor."

What former Mountie won a Victoria Cross in the Boer War?

Arthur Richardson joined the North West Mounted Police after emigrating from England. At the outbreak of the Boer War, he enlisted with the Lord Strathcona Horse and was sent to South Africa. In an engagement at Wolwespruit on July 5, 1900, Richardson saw that a wounded comrade who was pinned under his fallen horse was in danger of being killed or captured. Though he himself was sick with a fever, Richardson rode to the man's aid. With bullets whistling around him, Richardson pulled the soldier from under the horse, draped him over his own saddle, and dashed to safety. This act of selfless courage earned Richardson the Victoria Cross.

Quickies
Did you know ...
- that in the Boer War battle of Liliefontein on November 17, 1900, three Canadians: Hampden Churchill of Toronto, Edward Holland of Ottawa, and Richard Turner of Quebec City, all members of the Royal Canadian Dragoons, won the Victoria Cross for preventing the enemy from capturing two artillery pieces? One of those big guns can be seen at the Canadian War Museum in Ottawa.

What Canadian soldier won The Queen's Scarf of Honour in the Boer War?

Richard Rowland Thompson was a medical orderly attached to the Royal Canadian Regiment. He was originally from Ireland, but had immigrated to Canada and was living in Ottawa at the time he enlisted. During the Battle of Paardeberg in 1900, on several occasions Thompson crawled out into the deadly no man's land between the Canadian and Boer lines to treat wounded Canadian soldiers who had fallen on the battlefield. For repeatedly risking his own life to assist others, Thompson was twice recommended for the Victoria Cross, but both times his case was "not recognized." However, Queen Victoria had personally knitted eight woolen ceremonial scarves, each embroidered with a silk Royal Cipher. These prestigious and unique awards were to be given to soldiers from the ranks (not officers) who had distinguished themselves but had not received the Victoria Cross. Four of the scarves were to go to British soldiers. The other four were to be divided among the Canadian, Australian, New Zealand, and Cape Colony forces fighting in South Africa. Richard Rowland Thompson was chosen as the Canadian recipient. Thompson died of appendicitis in 1908 at the age of 31. His grave is at Chelsea, Quebec. His Scarf of Honour is on display at the Royal Canadian Regiment Museum in Ottawa.

Why is Georgina Pope included in the Valiants Memorial?

Georgina Pope of Prince Edward Island was a nurse who served with distinction in the Boer War and the First World War. In 1902, she was made a commander of the Canadian Army Nursing Service. In 1903, she was the first Canadian to be awarded the Royal Red Cross. In 1908, she was appointed First Matron of the Canadian Army Medical Corps.

Where did the Canadian Expeditionary Force (CEF) fight in the First World War?

The Canadians fought on the Western Front in France and Flanders, a region of Belgium. From Gravenstafel in April of 1915, to Mons in 1918, the CEF was engaged in 48 battles, including such major campaigns as the Somme, Ypres, Vimy Ridge, Hill 70, Passchendaele, Amiens, and Cambrai. A First World War battle could last for hours, days, weeks, or months. In between battles the soldiers endured the misery of life in the trenches and the constant sniping that went on between the opposing lines.

Who was the first Canadian to win a Victoria Cross in the First World War?

Originally from Ireland, Michael O'Leary immigrated to Canada and joined the North West Mounted Police. During the First World War he served with the Irish Guards. On February 1, 1915, Lance Corporal O'Leary single-handedly stormed an enemy barricade. He killed five Germans, and then assaulted a second barricade where he killed three more Germans and took two others prisoner. O'Leary was awarded the Victoria Cross, and the newspapers called his action "the greatest deed of the war." Poems and ballads were written about it, and O'Leary's wax effigy was an attraction in Madame Tussaud's. After the war, O'Leary returned to Canada and joined the Ontario Provincial Police.

Quickies

Did you know ...

- that before the Battle of Ypres in 1915, the German officers contemptuously dismissed the soldiers of the CEF as "clodhoppers"? By the time the battle was over they had to admit that the Canadians were a tough fighting force. Four Canadians who fought at Ypres were awarded the Victoria Cross, two of them posthumously. The carnage at Ypres inspired Lieutenant Colonel John McCrae of Guelph, Ontario, a field surgeon with the medical corps, to write his famous poem, "In Flanders Fields."

Why was the Canadian Expeditionary Force called "the Salvation Army" in 1915?

During the First World War, the situation on the Western Front had bogged down into the stalemate of trench warfare by 1915. In April, at Ypres in Belgium, the German army attempted to break through the Allied lines by using poison gas. French troops fled, leaving a four-mile-wide gap in the Allied lines which the Germans quickly tried to exploit. In spite of the deadly gas, the Canadians closed the gap and held the line until reinforcements could arrive. This was the first major First

World War battle in which Canadian troops participated. They saved the day, but at a cost of 6,035 lives.

Why does Vimy Ridge have a special place in Canadian military history?

Vimy Ridge is an escarpment in France that the Germans occupied early in the war. It was a strategic high ground that the Allies desperately wanted to take back. French and British attacks had been utter failures. In a battle lasting from April 9 to April 12, 1917, the Canadian Corps under Lieutenant General Sir Julian Byng succeeded where the British and French had failed, and captured Vimy Ridge. The operation had been meticulously planned, and the soldiers thoroughly trained for the jobs they were to do — something almost unheard of in the Allied armies up to that time. Nonetheless, the fighting was savage. The Canadians had 3,600 killed, 7,000 wounded, and 400 missing in action. It has been said that the young Canadian nation "came of age" on Vimy Ridge. The capture of Vimy Ridge was the first important Allied victory after more than two years of stalemate on the Western Front.

Quickies
Did you know ...
- that four Canadians were awarded the Victoria Cross for bravery shown at Vimy Ridge? They were: Captain Thain MacDowell of Maitland, Ontario; Private Bill Milne, a Manitoban who was originally from Scotland; Sergeant Ellis Sifton of Wallacetown, Ontario; and Private John Pattison of Calgary. Only Captain MacDowell lived to receive his decoration. The others were all awarded posthumously. A mountain in Jasper National Park, Alberta, has been named in John Pattison's honour.

What happened at Passchendaele?

The Battle of Passchendaele, in which the Allies' goal was to capture the village of that name, was actually a series of battles that began in June of 1917, and ended that November. In the final phase it was the Canadians who finally captured the high ground on which the ruins of

Ten Canadians Awarded the Victoria Cross After Passchendale

- Lieutenant Colonel Philip Bent, Halifax, Nova Scotia (posthumously)
- Private Tom Holmes, Owen Sound, Ontario.
- Captain Christopher O'Kelly, Winnipeg, Manitoba
- Lieutenant Robert Shankland, Winnipeg
- Private Cecil Kinross, Lougheed, Alberta
- Sergeant George Mullin, Moosomin, Saskatchewan.
- Lieutenant Hugh McKenzie, originally from Liverpool, immigrated to Canada, (posthumously)
- Major George Randolph Pearks, Red Deer, Alberta
- Private James P. Robertson, Medicine Hat, Alberta, (posthumously)
- Corporal Collin Barron, Toronto, Ontario

Passchendaele sat. Passchendaele was the epitome of everything that was terrible about the First World War: a sea of mud, foul trenches, incompetent generalship, and soldiers dying by the thousands for a few yards of worthless ground. The Allies lost half a million men at Passchendaele, 15,654 of the casualties being Canadian. The Germans lost 350,000.

What future governor general of Canada was a decorated as a First World War hero?

Georges Vanier of Montreal was an officer in the first exclusively French Canadian regiment of the Canadian Army, the Royal 22e Regiment. This regiment would become famous as the Van Doos, a corruption of *vingt-deuxième*. During his many months in the foul trenches of the Western Front, Vanier saw plenty of action, was promoted from lieutenant to captain, received the Military Cross and the French *Légion d'honneur* for bravery. In June 1916, he was wounded in battle and sent to a hospital in England. Two months later he was back at the front. In 1917, he fought at Hill 70 and Passchendaele. In the summer and autumn of 1918, Vanier was part of Canada's "Hundred Days," when Canadian troops spearheaded the Allied advance that resulted in Germany's defeat. Vanier was shot through the body, and had one leg so badly mangled by shrapnel it had to be amputated above the knee. Vanier had a Bar added to his Military Cross, and was awarded the Distinguished Service Order by King George V. After the war, Georges Vanier had a stellar diplomatic career, and in 1959 became Canada's first French Canadian governor general.

Who was the first Canadian fighter pilot to shoot down an enemy plane in the First World War?

On December 19, 1915, Malcolm McBean Bell-Irving was attacked by three German planes while flying on patrol over the Western Front. He shot one plane down and drove the other two away, and then was wounded by anti-aircraft fire. Bell-Irving was awarded the Distinguished Service Order (DSO).

Quickies
Did you know ...
- that during the Second World War, Georges Vanier and his wife Pauline were among the first people in Western diplomatic circles to acknowledge and condemn Nazi atrocities? They championed the cause of war refugees, even though xenophobic and anti-Semitic policies of the Canadian government shut Canada's doors to all but a trickle of European refugees.

Who was the top Canadian air ace in the First World War?

William Avery "Billy" Bishop of Owen Sound, Ontario, is on record for scoring 72 air victories. That's not counting the three observation balloons he destroyed. Bishop once engaged in an aerial dogfight with the legendary Red Baron, Manfred von Richthofen, though neither was able to shoot the other down. On June 2, 1917, Bishop single-handedly attacked a German airfield and downed three enemy planes, for which he was awarded the Victoria Cross. The Germans actually had a bounty on Billy Bishop's head. They called him "Hell's Handmaiden."

Quickies
Did you know ...
- that before First World War planes were fitted with machine guns, enemy pilots flying reconnaissance would blast away at each other with handguns and shotguns? Malcolm McBean Bell-Irving once tried to shoot an enemy pilot with a revolver. The gun misfired, so Bell-Irving threw it at the German, hitting him on the side of the head.

What type of plane did Billy Bishop fly?

Bishop scored most of his victories in a Nieuport 17 biplane. He painted the front of it blue so he'd be camouflaged against the sky.

What Canadian fighter pilot was credited with killing the Red Baron?

On the morning of April 21, 1918, Royal Air Force 209 Squadron got into a dogfight with the legendary Flying Circus of Manfred Von Richtofen, the much-feared Red Baron. Novice Canadian pilot Wilfrid "Wop" May pulled out of the scrap because his machine guns were jammed. The Red Baron spotted him and swooped down for the kill. Flight Commander Arthur "Roy" Brown, of Carlton Place, Ontario, saw May in trouble, and dove after the Red Baron, firing a burst from his guns. This forced the Red Baron to break off his attack on May. He then seemed to pursue May again before gliding his plane to a landing in a field behind Allied lines. Australian soldiers found Von Richtofen sitting in the cockpit, dead from a single bullet. The Royal Air Force credited Captain Brown with killing the Red Baron and awarded him the Distinguished Service Cross. However, an Australian anti-aircraft gun crew had also been shooting at Von Richtofen's plane and they claimed it was their bullet that killed the German ace. The controversy continues to this day.

Ten Other Canadian First World War Air Aces and Their Scores

- Raymond Collishaw — 62
- Donald Maclaren — 54
- William Barker — 53
- Alfred Atkey — 38
- Frederick McCall — 37
- William Claxton — 36
- Joseph Fall — 36
- Francis G. Quigly — 34
- Albert "Nick" Carter — 31
- Andrew McKeever — 30

Who commanded the Black Flight?

Flight Commander Raymond Collishaw of Nanaimo, British Columbia, an officer in the Royal Naval Air Service, commanded No. 10 Naval Squadron. The five-man Canadian squadron all flew Sopwith Triplanes, which they painted jet black and gave ominous names. Collishaw had the second highest number of air victories among Canadian First World

War fighter pilots, second only to Billy Bishop, but he never received Bishop's level of publicity. Collishaw's military decorations included: Commander of the Order of the Bath, Order of the British Empire, Distinguished Service Order and bar, Distinguished Service Cross, Distinguished Flying Cross,

> **The Pilots of the Black Flight and Their Planes**
> - Raymond Collishaw — *Black Maria*
> - J.E. Sharmon — *Black Death*
> - Ellis Reid — *Black Roger*
> - Marcus Alexander — *Black Prince*
> - Gerry Nash — *Black Sheep*

and the *Croix de Guerre* of France. Collishaw also fought against the Bolsheviks in the Russian Civil War, and served in the Second World War as an air vice marshal.

What was unusual about the Victoria Crosses won by Lieutenant Fred Harvey of Alberta, Lieutenant Harcus Strachan of Winnipeg, and Lieutenant Gordon Flowerdew of Saskatchewan during the First World War?

These three Canadians were awarded the Victoria Cross (Flowerdew posthumously) for extreme courage displayed in cavalry charges. In a conflict that quickly bogged down into trench warfare, cavalry was useless. The dramatic, romantic cavalry charge of an earlier day was obsolete. However, on a few occasions the horse soldiers did get the opportunity to ride for glory.

What act of heroism earned Corporal Joseph Kaeble the Victoria Cross?

On June 8, 1918, at Neuville-Vitasse, France, everyone in Corporal Kaeble's section had been killed or wounded, leaving him to face a German advance alone. Holding his Lewis gun at the hip, he emptied one magazine after another into the Germans and drove back the attack. He was wounded several times, but continued to shoot at the retreating Germans. He died the following day in hospital. Kaeble was posthumously awarded the Victoria Cross "for most conspicuous bravery and extraordinary devotion to duty."

Who were the first men of the Royal Canadian Navy to be killed in the First World War?

Canada did not have much of a navy at the beginning of the First World War, but it did have men in training on some old, cast-off Royal Navy cruisers. In August 1914, the Royal Navy cruiser HMS *Good Hope* docked at Halifax to take on fuel. Four midshipmen from the first graduating class of the Royal Naval College of Canada were taken aboard as crewmen: Malcolm Cann, John Hatheway, William Palmer, and Arthur Silver. On November 1, the *Good Hope* engaged the German cruisers *Gneisenau* and *Scharnhorst* off the coast of Chile. The *Good Hope* was destroyed and went down with all hands. The four Canadians were the first of 225 Canadian seamen who were killed on British ships during the war.

Who was the only Canadian navy man to win a Victoria Cross in the First World War?

Rowland Bourke was a Royal Naval Volunteer Reserve officer in command of a motor launch participating in the blockade of the port of Ostend, Belgium. On May 10, 1918, Bourke went into the harbour to pick up survivors from the crippled British war ship *Vindictive*. In spite of heavy enemy machine-gun fire, Bourke and his crew pulled three British seamen out of the water and took them to safety.

Why is there a monument to the memory of Hugh Cairns in a park in Saskatoon, Saskatchewan?

Sergeant Hugh Cairns of Saskatoon was the last Canadian to be awarded the Victoria Cross in the First World War. On November 2, 1918, less than a fortnight before the November 11 armistice, Cairns single-handedly knocked out a German machine-gun position, killing 12 Germans and capturing 18 more. Later that same day, Cairns outflanked another German position, killed several of them and captured 50. He then entered a barn where another 60 Germans surrendered to him. However, as they filed out, an officer pulled a revolver and shot Cairns in the stomach. Cairns died the next day, and was awarded the Victoria Cross posthumously.

Who was the most decorated Canadian in the First World War?

A fighter pilot, Lieutenant Colonel William Barker of Dauphin, Manitoba, was Canada's most decorated war hero. He was awarded the Victoria Cross, the Military Cross and two bars, the Distinguished Service Order and bar, France's Croix de Guerre, and Italy's Valore Militare.

What distinction did the Royal Newfoundland Regiment have in the First World War?

The Royal Newfoundland Regiment was the only North American regiment to fight in the disastrous Gallipoli campaign of 1915. Later, on July 1, 1916, during the Battle of the Somme, the Royal Newfoundland Regiment was almost annihilated at a place called Beaumont Hamel. Lieutenant Colonel Arthur Lovell Hadow made the observation that the Newfoundlanders' attack failed because "dead men can advance no further." This massive loss of men from a colony with a small population had a profound effect on Newfoundland's history and culture. Today Newfoundland's Memorial Day is July 1.

Quickies

Did you know ...

- Private Thomas Ricketts, age 17, of the Royal Newfoundland Regiment, was the youngest person ever to be awarded the Victoria Cross? There is a memorial to Ricketts, who died in 1967, on Water Street in St. John's. A play about him, *The Known Soldier*, was written by Jeff Pitcher.

Where did the Canadian Armed Forces fight in the Second World War?

Canada's military forces were much more diversified in the Second World War than they had been in the First World War, and the Second World War was much more of a global conflict. Canadian naval vessels participated in actions on both the Atlantic and the Pacific Oceans. Canadian ground troops were involved in hundreds of operations, large and small, from a raid on Norway's Spitzbergen Islands, to the major campaigns in Italy, France, Belgium, the Netherlands, and Germany. Canadians also fought in Hong Kong and Southeast Asia. Canadian airmen, flying with the Royal Canadian Air Force or the Royal Air Force saw action as fighter and bomber pilots and crewmen in every theatre of the war.

Who was the first Canadian to be decorated in the Second World War?

Robert Timbrell of Vancouver had joined the Royal Canadian Navy in 1937 and in 1940 was in England for training with the Royal Navy. From May 27 to June 4 of that year he participated in the "Miracle of Dunkirk" in which thousands of British and French soldiers were evacuated from French beaches before they could be slaughtered or captured by an advancing German army. Captain Timbrell was placed in command of HMS *Llanthony,* a civilian yacht with no armament that was just one of the hastily assembled fleet thrown together for the evacuation. Timbrell distinguished himself by taking men off the Dunkirk beach under heavy fire, ferrying them to England, and then going back for more. Even though his vessel had taken some hits and five of his crew were killed, Timbrell was placed in command of a flotilla of four trawlers, one of which was lost to a mine. For his courage and resourcefulness, Timbrell received the Distinguished Service Cross, the first decoration won by any Canadian in the Second World War.

Who was the first Canadian Second World War pilot to achieve the status of ace?

To be called an ace, a fighter pilot had to shoot down at least five enemy planes. The first Canadian to do that was Angus Benjamin of Winnipeg. On May 10, 1940, he shot down his first German plane. On May 12 he got two more. Benjamin achieved ace status on May 14 when two more German planes went down before the guns of his Hurricane fighter. Sadly, on May 16, Benjamin was killed in action. He was posthumously awarded the Distinguished Flying Cross.

Why was Second World War fighter pilot George Beurling nicknamed "Buzz"?

Actually, Beurling's fellow pilots called him "Screwball"! George Beurling of Verdun, Quebec, was insubordinate and a major discipline problem to his superior officers. But at the controls of a Spitfire fighter plane he was a daredevil pilot with uncanny marksmanship. Beurling was a master of the "deflection shot." He could calculate in an instant where an enemy plane was going to be, and then send off a stream of machine-gun bullets that the target plane would fly right into. In the Battle of Malta in 1942, Beurling shot down 27 enemy planes. Beurling's official wartime tally was 31, for which he received the Distinguished Service Order, the Distinguished Flying Medal with a bar for bravery, and the Distinguished Flying Cross. When Beurling reluctantly returned to Canada to promote war bonds, the government did not think "Screwball" was an appropriate nickname for a war hero. Thus, he became known to the Canadian public as "Buzz."

Quickies

Did you know ...

- after the Second World War, Buzz Beurling could not find steady work as a pilot? In 1948 he enlisted with the Israeli Air Force, and then was killed in a mysterious plane crash at the age of 27.

How many Canadian airmen participated in the Battle of Britain?

In the summer and autumn of 1940 the German *Luftwaffe* attempted to gain control of the skies over Britain and bomb the British people into submission. Its failure to accomplish either objective was Nazi Germany's first defeat and a major turning point in the war. In what Winston Churchill called Britain's "finest hour," 110 Canadians flew the Hurricanes and Spitfires that turned back the Nazi tide. Three of the Canadian pilots were awarded the Distinguished Flying Cross.

Why was J.F. "Stocky" Edwards called "The Desert Hawk"?

James Francis "Stocky" Edwards of Nokomis, Saskatchewan, was posted to the Middle East after completing his pilot training, and on his first operational flight he shot down a Messerschmitt 109. Stocky Edwards continued to roll up his score of enemy planes. Even though he was pulled out of combat for six months to do duty as a gunnery instructor, by the end of the Desert War he was the number one desert air force ace with 11 planes shot down (confirmed), eight more probably destroyed, five damaged in the air, and several destroyed or damaged on the ground. Edwards also fought in the campaigns in Italy and Normandy. In addition to enemy aircraft destroyed or damaged, he destroyed or damaged some 300 ground vehicles. Wing Commander Edwards was awarded the Distinguished Flying Cross with Bar and the Distinguished Flying Medal. He later received the Order of Canada.

Why were Canadian troops sent to defend Hong Kong?

The British high command had already decided that it would be impossible to defend Hong Kong in the face of a sustained Japanese attack. Hong Kong had no naval protection and no worthwhile air cover. However, the generals thought that the addition of 2,000 Canadian troops to the garrison would deter the Japanese from attacking. Canadian prime minister Mackenzie King believed sending the Canadians to Hong Kong would be a unifying factor, since one battalion, the Winnipeg Grenadiers, was from the West, and the other, the Royal Rifles of Canada, was from Quebec City.

What happened when the Japanese attacked Hong Kong?

On December 8, 1941, 52,000 Japanese troops attacked Hong Kong, which was defended by 14,000 British, Canadian, and Indian troops. The fighting lasted until December 25. In spite of being outnumbered, ill equipped, and poorly trained, the Canadians fought well against battle-hardened, well-equipped Japanese troops. The Canadians had 290 killed and 493 wounded. Another 267 Canadians would die as prisoners of war in brutal slave camps.

Why is August 9, 1942, considered one of the darkest days in Canadian military history?

August 9, 1942, was the date of the raid in the French coastal town of Dieppe,

Twelve Canadians Who Were Decorated for Actions During the Battle of Hong Kong

- Major Wells Arnold Bishop — Distinguished Service Order
- Captain Robert W. Philip — Military Cross
- Lieutenant Thomas A. Blackwood — Military Cross
- Quartermaster Sergeant Colin A. Standish — Distinguished Conduct Medal
- Lieutenant Collinson Blaver — Military Cross
- Corporal Derek Rix — Distinguished Conduct Medal
- Sergeant Major John W. Osborne — Victoria Cross
- Captain Frederick Atkinson — Military Cross
- Major Ernest Hodkinson — Distinguished Service Order
- Chaplain (Honorary Captain) Uriah Laite — Military Cross
- Lieutenant Francis G. Power — Military Cross
- Lieutenant William F. Nugent — Military Cross

33

which was carried out by an almost all-Canadian force. Code-named Jubilee, the operation was supposed to be a surprise attack. Far from being surprised, the German defenders were ready and waiting. The Canadians had 913 killed, 586 wounded among those who made it back to England, and 1,946 taken prisoner.

What was the purpose of the Dieppe raid?

The operation was the brainchild of Lord Mountbatten. (General Montgomery was against it). The attackers were supposed to seize the town and hold it long enough for engineers to destroy the harbour facilities and some German military installations, as well as take some prisoners and German military documents. The Western Allies had also been under pressure from Soviet premier Josef Stalin to open up a front in the west to take some of the pressure off the embattled Red Army in the east.

Why did the Dieppe raid fail?

All element of surprise was lost when the flotilla encountered a small German convoy in the English Channel. There was no preliminary aerial or naval bombardment, and air and naval support was insufficient. The attack fell behind schedule, and landings that were supposed to have been made under cover of darkness were made in daylight. When tanks went ashore, their treads were quickly fouled by the stony beaches which not only stopped them from advancing, but made them sitting targets for German guns. The defending German 571st Infantry Regiment was well-trained, well-equipped, and positioned on heights that enabled them to slaughter the Canadians as they came ashore. The landing craft proved unsuitable for evacuating the men under fire, hence the large number of prisoners.

Who was "The Gallant Padre"?

Among the many Canadians who were decorated for their actions at Dieppe was Regimental Chaplain John Weir Foote of Madoc, Ontario. At Dieppe, Foote was an assistant in the Regimental Aid Post, helping the medical officer tend to the wounded. He consistently exposed himself to enemy gunfire in order to administer morphine or carry wounded men to the medical post. As the raid became a disaster, Foote helped to load wounded men into the landing craft. Foote was in the last boat as it was about to leave, when he did one of the most unselfish deeds of the day. He left the craft and walked back up the beach to be taken prisoner, so that he could console and minister to the many young men who had been captured. Upon his liberation from a POW camp in April 1945, Foote was awarded the Victoria Cross. He was the only member of the Canadian Chaplain Services ever to receive the honour.

What was the legacy of Dieppe?

The legacy of Dieppe has been a bitter one. To this day many people believe the Germans were tipped off about the attack. Many felt that Lord Mountbatten was not a competent military man, and that he used the Canadians as guinea pigs to test German coastal defences. However, lessons learned at Dieppe contributed to the success of amphibious landings elsewhere, particularly at Normandy in June 1944. In September 1944, the 2nd Canadian Infantry was sent to liberate Dieppe. The Germans occupying the town fled without a fight.

Quickies

Did you know ...

- that 50 American Rangers, the first Americans to fight in Europe in the Second World War, were at Dieppe? Three of them were killed. Back in England, the surviving Rangers were all awarded medals by Lord Mountbatten. He had no similar decoration for the surviving Canadians.

Why is Captain John Wallace Thomas included in the Valiants Memorial?

Captain Thomas of Newfoundland is representative of the service performed by the men of the merchant marine. He served with distinction in both world wars. In 1940 he was made Commander of the British Empire for his courage and resourcefulness in handling his ship, the *Empress of Scotland,* during a Luftwaffe attack off the coast of Ireland. Captain Thomas was the only member of the Canadian merchant navy to be awarded the CBE during the war.

What native of Prince Edward Island participated in an action described as "one of the greatest episodes in naval history"?

Frederick Thornton Peters was born in Prince Edward Island in 1889. He served as a junior officer in the Royal Navy during the First World War and was twice decorated. On November 8, 1942, during the Second World War, Captain Peters was with the British-American raid on the port of Oran, Algeria. The objective was the capture or destruction of French warships that were part of the armed forces of the Vichy French government, which was collaborating with the Nazis. The Allies hoped that the French servicemen would defy their traitorous Vichy officers and give no resistance. Instead, the French put up a stiff fight, and the Allied operation seemed doomed to failure. Captain Peters was in command of two cutters. In an act of almost suicidal bravery, he rammed the log boom across the harbour entrance and broke through. French warships opened fire on the cutters from point-blank range, destroying them both and killing most of the crewmen. Peters survived, but lost an eye and was taken prisoner. British ships sank or captured all of the French vessels attempting to escape. Two days later Peters was freed from jail by American soldiers. When local people learned he was the officer who had led the charge into the harbour, they carried him through the streets on their shoulders and showered him with flowers. One day later a plane carrying Peters to England crashed into the sea. No bodies were recovered. Frederick Peters was posthumously awarded the Victoria Cross and the United States Distinguished Service Cross. A Naval Reserve building in Charlottetown was named in his honour.

Who was one of the first Allied soldiers to go ashore in the invasion of Sicily?

In the British/Canadian/American landings on Sicily on July 10, 1943, one of the first men ashore was General Guy Granville Simonds of the First Canadian Infantry Division. For the invasion of mainland Italy on September 3, 1943, General Simmonds was given command of the Fifth Armoured Canadian Division. He later led the First Canadian Army in Belgium during the Battle of the Scheldt. General Bernard Montgomery, the senior British commander, called General Simonds the "most brilliant Canadian field general." Simonds was awarded the Commander of the Order of the Bath, Commander of the Order of the British Empire, and the Distinguished Service Order.

Who was the only French-Canadian soldier to be awarded the Victoria Cross in the Second World War?

On December 14, 1943, at Casa Berardi, Italy, Major Paul Triquet of Cabano, Quebec, and his men captured a three storey farmhouse that was a key to securing a road junction. They had to knock out four German tanks and a machine-gun nest, and then hold the position against superior numbers until relief could come. All of the Canadian officers except Triquet were killed or wounded, and the unit lost 50 percent of its men. Triquet's courage and leadership inspired the rest of the men to hold on. In addition to the Victoria Cross, Triquet was also awarded the French *Légion d'honneur*.

What was "The Devil's Brigade"?

The First Special Service Force was an elite, specially trained commando unit made of Canadian and American soldiers. Originally intended to fight the Japanese in the Aleution Islands, they were used on special operations in Italy and France in 1943 and 1944. Because the commandos often operated at night with their faces blackened with boot polish, the Germans called them *Die schwarzen Teufel* — the black devils. They would tag demolished German military property and dead German soldiers with labels that said in German, "The worst is yet to come." The 1968 movie *The Devil's Brigade* starring William Holden and Cliff Robertson was loosely based on the First Special Service Force's story.

Who was the most decorated member of the Devil's Brigade?

Thomas Prince, an Ojibwa from Petersfield, Manitoba, was the most decorated member of the Devil's Brigade and one of the most decorated Canadians. His nine military awards included a Military Medal presented to him by King George V, and the American Silver Star. A statue of Tommy Prince was erected in a Winnipeg park in 1989.

Quickies
Did you know ...
* Tommy Prince was honourably discharged from the Canadian army in June 1945? When the Korean War broke out in 1950, Prince re-enlisted in spite of suffering from arthritis in his knees, and became a member of Princess Patricia's Light Infantry, the famed Princess Pats. Prince served with distinction in Korea, was wounded in action, and was honourably discharged a second time.

Who was the real "Tunnel King" in the true story of the Great Escape?

Canadian fighter pilot Wally Floody had worked in the mines of Northern Ontario, so when he wound up as a prisoner of war in Stalag Luft III after being shot down over France in 1941, he had the very skills the camp's escape committee was looking for. Floody was the principal architect and digger of the tunnels that were dug as part of a major break-out attempt. However, Floody did not get a chance to get out on the night of the escape. The German guards became suspicious a few days before the event and transferred Floody to another POW camp. Floody returned to Canada after the war and was later employed as a technical advisor on the set of the 1963 film *The Great Escape*.

Quickies
Did you know ...

- that, of the 79 men who got out of Stalag Luft III during the Great Escape, only three made it to neutral countries? The other 76 were re-captured. Fifty of the re-captured escapees were shot on Hitler's orders. They included six Canadians: Henry Birkland, Gordon Kidder, Patrick Langford, George McGill, James Wernham, and George Wiley. Three other Canadians who escaped were recaptured but were not murdered: Bill Cameron, Keith Ogilvie, and Alfred Thompson.

How did the Canadians break through the Hitler Line?

In May of 1944, the Allied advance up the Italian peninsula was held up by the much vaunted Adolf Hitler Line, the most formidable German fortification they had yet encountered. This was a concentration of concrete heavy gun and rocket emplacements that ran from Aquino in the east to Pontecorvo in the west. When the Canadians finally penetrated this barrier, Division Commander Christopher Vokes gave credit for the breakthrough to the First Canadian Division's chief gunner, William S. Ziegler. The artillery officer and his staff worked 72 hours without a break, planning and executing their barrage. It was one of the most complex artillery fire plans ever conceived of, and it was the heaviest of the Second World War up to that time. It consisted of a series of concentrated fire on specific targets, and a creeping barrage that moved 900 feet every three minutes. All this was accompanied by a relentless fire of a thousand shells per hour. When the Canadians were held up in the Aquino sector, Zeigler took less than half an hour to improvise a new plan that called for 668 guns to throw 3,509 shells on the enemy. The Hitler Line collapsed. When the battle was over, Zeigler reluctantly drank a glass of Canadian rye whiskey Vokes thrust upon him, and then passed out after having gone three days without sleep.

Who was the first member of the Royal Canadian Air Force to be awarded the Victoria Cross?

On June 24, 1944, Flight Lieutenant David "Bud" Hornell of Mimico, Ontario, flying a Catalina anti-submarine bomber, attacked a German U-boat about 1,000 miles from his base in the Shetland Islands. The sub was running on the surface, and the crew of its deck gun opened fire on Hornell's plane. The aircraft was hit several times and was on fire, but Hornell pressed on with the attack and destroyed the U-boat. Then he had to ditch the plane in the ocean. Hornell and all seven of his crew got out before the plane sank, but only one of their two dinghies inflated properly. The other one exploded. The dinghy could hold only seven, so the men had to take turns going into the frigid water and hanging on. Hornell voluntarily spent more time in the water than any of his men. The dinghy was spotted by the pilot of another Catalina, but many hours passed before a rescue vessel could reach the men. One crew member became delirious from exposure and died. Heavy seas kept swamping the dinghy, and the survivors had to bail constantly. A Warwick transport plane dropped a lifeboat, but high winds carried it away. Hornell, who by now was weak from seasickness and almost blind from the effects of exposure, wanted to swim after it but his men held him back. Throughout the ordeal, Hornell encouraged the men not to give up hope. After the survivors endured 21 hours on the cruel North Sea, a launch picked them up. By that time Hornell was unconscious. He died within a few hours. Hornell was buried in a military cemetery in the Shetland Islands, and was posthumously awarded the Victoria Cross.

How did Andrew Mynarski receive a belated, posthumous Victoria Cross?

Warrant Officer Mynarski was a gunner aboard a Lancaster bomber that was part of a raid on the railyards of Cambrai, France, on the night of June 12–13, 1944. As the plane was about to make its bombing run, it was attacked by a German fighter. Both port engines were knocked out and a fire started inside the plane. The pilot ordered the crew to bail out. Most of the men got out, but when Mynarski reached the escape hatch, he saw that his friend, rear gunner Pat Brophy, was trapped in his turret. Mynarski crawled through flames to reach Brophy and try to get the turret open, but it wouldn't budge. By now his own clothes and parachute pack were on fire. Brophy shouted at Mynarski to get out while he had the chance. Mynarski crawled back to the escape hatch, turned and saluted Brophy, and then jumped from the plane. French farmers saw Mynarski come down because his clothes and parachute were still on fire. When they found him he was badly burned and seriously injured from his impact with the ground. He was taken to a German field hospital where he died. Meanwhile, when the Lancaster crashed, Brophy's turret was thrown aside and he escaped relatively unhurt. He was hidden by the French Resistance and assisted them in their war against the Germans until September 1944 when the area was liberated by the British. Not until Brophy got back to England was he able to report the story of Mynarski's unselfish courage. Mynarski was awarded the Victoria Cross in 1946.

What was the Canadian army's role in the D-Day invasion of Normandy?

The Canadians were to land on the beach code named Juno, which was defended by the German army's 716th division. This was not considered a top German division, though its position was well fortified and strengthened with 90 big guns, 50 mortars, and from 400 to 500 machine guns. However, nearby were two tough German armoured formations: the 21st Panzer Division near Caen, and the 12th SS Panzer Division a few miles farther inland. The Canadians and their British allies who had been assigned Gold and Sword beaches were to push inland and seize Caen and Bayeux, as well as the roads and rails connecting them, and prepare for a German armoured counter-offensive.

How well did the Canadian army do on D-Day?

Although the Canadians and British failed to capture Caen until later in the Normandy Campaign, on D-Day the Canadians pushed farther inland than any of the other Allied armies. This was done at a cost of 1,074 casualties, which included 335 dead. This was a lighter casualty rate than had been expected, but it increased as the Canadians pushed farther inland and German resistance stiffened.

Why did the Canadians have a special hatred for Colonel Kurt Meyer of the Waffen SS?

In the fighting around Caen, Meyer commanded three infantry battalions and one tank battalion. He gave orders that no Allied prisoners were to be taken. As a result, 134 Canadians who had been captured were murdered in cold blood. After the war, Meyer was tried as a war criminal for 27 of the murders. He was found guilty and sentenced to hang, but the death sentence was commuted to life imprisonment. He was released in 1954.

How did a cigarette case save the life of *Star Trek*'s "Scotty" during the Normandy Campaign?

Vancouver-born James Doohan stormed Juno Beach with the Canadian army on D-Day, and allegedly helped knock out a German machine gun. A few days after the landing, as his regiment advanced into Normandy, Doohan was hit by machine-gun fire. He received bullet wounds in his leg and right hand. Another bullet struck him in the chest and could have been fatal, but was deflected by a metal cigarette case in his pocket. As a result of the injury to his right hand, Doohan had the middle finger amputated. Years later, when Doohan played Chief Engineer Montgomery Scott of the Starship *Enterprise,* the TV show's producers took care to hide Scotty's disfigured hand from viewers. In close-up shots of Scotty's hands working the controls of the transporter, "stand-in" hands were used. In the episode "Trouble with Tribbles," when both of Scott's hands are in view while he holds a pile of the creatures, his missing finger is supposedly buried in tribble fur.

How did a Canadian fighter pilot knock Germany's top general out of the war?

Charley Fox of Guelph, Ontario, had already participated in the Battle of Britain, flown in the D-Day invasion of Normandy, attacked V1 and V2 rocket-launching sites, and earned the Distinguished Flying Cross and Bar, when he performed one of the most important single acts of the war.

Quickies
Did you know ...
- D-Day was the first time the Canadian army fought under the Red Ensign? Before that, Canadians had fought under the British Union Jack.

On July 17, 1944, Fox was flying across the French countryside looking for "targets of opportunity" when he spotted a German military staff car racing along a tree-lined road. While his wing mate Steve Randall flew cover for him, Fox dove at the German car and strafed it. The car went off the road and rolled over. Allied intelligence later learned that Germany's top general, Field Marshal Erwin Rommel had suffered serious head injuries when his car was attacked by a fighter plane. Several pilots sought credit for strafing Rommel, but investigation eventually proved beyond a doubt that Charley Fox was the man who had put the legendary Desert Fox out of action. Fox had recorded the incident in his logbook, but never boasted of it. On October 18, 2008, at the age of 88, Charley Fox was killed in a car accident near Tillsonberg, Ontario.

Quickies
Did you know ...
- that on July 20, 1944, three days after Charley Fox shot up Rommel's car, German conspirators failed in an attempt to assassinate Adolf Hitler with a bomb? Nazi investigators believed Rommel was involved in the plot to kill Hitler and negotiate Germany's surrender to the Western Allies. To avoid Nazi persecution of his family, as well as the humiliation of a trial, Rommel committed suicide by means of poison on October 14, 1944. The Nazi government told the German people he had died as a result of the wounds he'd received when his car was strafed by a Spitfire.

What real-life Canadian master of espionage was a model for Ian Fleming's fictional character James Bond?

In the First World War, William Stephenson of Winnipeg was a decorated fighter pilot. In the Second World War very few people knew that he was one of the most important men in the Allied war effort. Working in a New York City office under the cover of British Passport Control Officer, Stephenson was secretly the head of an umbrella organization that included the British Intelligence agencies MI5 and MI6, the Secret Intelligence Service (SIS), the Special Operations Executive (SOE), and the Political Warfare Executive (PWE). Stephenson's operatives, most of whom knew him only by his code name, Intrepid, carried out espionage and counter-espionage activities in Europe, North and South America, and the Caribbean. He set up Camp X in Whitby on the shore of Lake Ontario east of Toronto as a training school for spies, saboteurs, and assassins. He was a close adviser to Winston Churchill and Franklin D. Roosevelt. After the war, Stephenson was knighted by King George VI. He was awarded the Presidential Medal for Merit, the highest American honour available to a civilian. Stephenson was the first non-American to receive that award. He was later made a Companion of the Order of Canada.

Quickies
Did you know ...
- five American graduates of William Stephenson's Camp X spy school went on to become directors of the Central Intelligence Agency (CIA)?

What three Canadians' names are on the Valencay SOE Memorial in France?

The Valencay Memorial honours all those Allied Special Operations men and women who lost their lives while carrying out extremely dangerous missions in Nazi-occupied France. The Canadian names on the Roll of Honour are Frank Herbert Pickersgill of Winnipeg, Romeo Sabourin of Montreal, and John Kenneth Macalister of Guelph, Ontario. These Canadian agents of Intrepid were captured by the Gestapo, brutally interrogated, and then executed by being hung on meat hooks and strangled with piano wire.

Who was the only woman to hold a senior position with SOE?

Kay Moore of Strathcona, Alberta, was studying at the Sorbonne in Paris when the Germans invaded France. She went to London, England, where she officially joined the First Aid Nursing Yeomanry (FANY), but was secretly working for SOE as an interpreter and liaison for Allied agents working behind enemy lines. One of those agents was her friend from the University of Manitoba, Frank Pickersgill. Kay Moore provided a vital link between the agents in the field and the British and American air forces that provided them with weapons and equipment. One of the resistance fighters she worked with was Ernest Gimpel (code name Charles Beauchamp), her future husband.

Quickies
Did you know ...
- that during one of his interrogation sessions, Frank Pickersgill grabbed a bottle, broke the neck, fatally stabbed an SS guard in the throat, and then jumped out a second storey window? He made a run for it but was cut down by bullets. The Nazis nursed him back to health in hope of extracting information from him. When they could get nothing out of him, they shipped him off to an extermination camp.

Who was the last Canadian to be awarded the Victoria Cross?

On August 9, 1945, Robert Hampton Gray, a native of Trail, British Columbia, was at the controls of a Vought Corsair fighter bomber. He was the flight commander of an eight-plane squadron that had taken off from the aircraft carrier HMS *Formidable* with orders to attack Japanese warships in Onagawa Bay. The Corsair carried two 500-pound bombs designed to be launched in a skip-bomb attack that assured maximum accuracy, but also left the low-flying plane dangerously

Quickies
Did you know ...
- that Kay Moore shared a London apartment with an art student from Toronto named Alison Grant who had become attached to Britain's Military Intelligence Sections 5 (MI5)? Their quarters, nicknamed the Canada House Annex, were approved as a "safe house" for agents about to go to the continent, or returning from a mission. Alison Grant would one day become the mother of Michael Ignatieff, leader of the Liberal Party of Canada.

vulnerable to anti-aircraft fire. Gray's target was the escort ship *Amakusa*. As he roared into the attack, anti-aircraft guns threw up a wall of fire. Gray's plane was hit several times and one of his bombs was knocked away. The Corsair was in flames, but Gray did not break off the attack or bail out. He waited until he was within 50 yards of the *Amakusa* before releasing his remaining bomb. It was a perfect hit amidships. Gray's plane then crashed into the sea. Neither the Corsair nor Gray's body was ever found. Gray was posthumously awarded the Victoria Cross, the last Canadian to receive that decoration. Only hours after Gray's heroic action, the Americans dropped the second atomic bomb on Japan, bringing the Second World War to an end.

Quickies

Did you know ...

- in 1989, the Japanese honoured Robert Gray with a cairn and a memorial plaque in Sakiyama Peace Park, which overlooks Onagawa Bay? It is the only memorial to a member of the Allied Forces on Japanese soil.

How many Canadians served in the Korean War?

Altogether 26,792 Canadians served in the Korean War. Of the 1,558 casualties, 516 were fatal. The names of the fallen are inscribed in the Korean Book of Remembrance.

How did the 2nd Princess Patricia's Canadian Light Infantry earn a United States Presidential Citation?

In a battle that lasted from April 23 to 25, 1951, the Princess Pats held a position in the valley of the Kapyong River against a massive Chinese attack. An Australian unit on the Canadians' flank was overwhelmed and forced to withdraw. At one point, the Canadians were entirely encircled by the enemy. However, they held on until the Chinese attack was broken and reserves could come to their assistance. While inflicting heavy losses on the enemy, the Princess Pats had 10 killed and 23 wounded. For this action the regiment was awarded the U.S. Presidential Citation.

Who was the only Canadian pilot shot down in the Korean War?

Andrew R. MacKenzie had been an air ace in the Second World War. In 1952 he went to Korea on an exchange basis with the Americans. On December 8, he was flying an F-86 Sabre fighter when he got into a dogfight with two North Korean MiGs. He was accidentally shot down by another American plane. MacKenzie bailed out and was captured by Chinese ground troops. He spent the next two years in a prison where he was brutally interrogated, subjected to brainwashing experiments, kept in solitary confinement for 465 days, and so poorly fed that he lost 70 pounds. He was released at the Hong Kong border on December 5, 1954. Mackenzie was awarded the Distinguished Flying Cross.

When did Canada officially dedicate the Tomb of the Unknown Soldier?

Though Canadians have a long tradition of honouring their country's war dead, it was not until May 28, 2000, that Canada officially had a Tomb of the Unknown Soldier. During a special ceremony the remains of an unknown Canadian soldier who had died in the Battle of Vimy Ridge in the First World War were laid to rest in a newly constructed sarcophagus in front of the National War Memorial in Ottawa. Tribute to the Unknown Soldier honours the many soldiers whose remains could not be identified when they were laid in their graves, or who do not have graves because their remains were never found.

How did two Canadian peacekeepers win the Star of Courage on Cyprus?

On July 20, 1974, Canadian peacekeeping soldiers found themselves in the middle of a shooting war between Greek and Turkish Cypriots. A Canadian officer, Captain Normand Blaquiere, was attempting to escort some Turks across the Pedhieos River, when Greeks opened fire on them. Four Turks were killed instantly and Blaquiere went down with bullets in both his legs. Private Michel Plouffe, who was assisting Blaquiere, threw himself across the captain to shield him from further fire. A bullet pierced Plouffe's helmet and shattered his jaw. Nonetheless, Plouffe continued to protect Blaquiere with his body. Captain Alain Forand saw the wounded

Canadians lying partially in the river and exposed to the Greek gunmen. He ordered the men in a Canadian observation post to provide him with covering fire. Then, with Greek bullets whistling around him, he dashed to the wounded men. One at a time he dragged them to safe cover. Captain Forand and Private Plouffe were both awarded the Star of Courage.

Where is Canada's Highway of Heroes?

On August 24, 2007, the Ministry of Transportation announced that the stretch of Highway 401 from Glen Miller Road in Trenton to the intersection of the Don Valley Parkway and Highway 404 in Toronto would be called Highway of Heroes in honour of Canadian Forces personnel killed in Afghanistan. This part of the highway is frequently the route of processions carrying a slain soldier's body from CFB Trenton to the coroner's office in Toronto. People line the overpasses to pay their respects as the processions pass by. Signs depicting a shield decorated with a poppy mark the Highway of Heroes.

**to serve
and protect**

Who was the first police officer in Canada to die in the line of duty?

The first known peace officer to die in the line of duty in Canada was High Constable John Fisk of York (Toronto). On October 7, 1804, he was aboard the schooner HMS *Speedy* escorting a murder suspect to the town of Newcastle to stand trial, when the vessel sank in a storm on Lake Ontario. There were no survivors.

Why is the Mountie seen as a heroic symbol of Canada?

Canada is not unique in having a police officer as a national symbol. The English bobby and the French *gendarme* are two examples of law enforcement figures being national icons. Nonetheless, the scarlet coated Mountie has been a romantic figure that has captured the public imagination from the very earliest days of the Force. The first Mounties rode out to a wild and wooly territory and quickly established themselves as the guardians of law and order. They did it without the excessive violence that was so common in the American West. Wild Bill Hickok and Wyatt Earp would not likely have been accepted as Mounties. With the exception of the events of the Northwest Rebellion in 1885, there were no major battles between companies of Mounties and Native warriors. Where the United States Army would send in a troop of cavalry to deal with Native issues, the North West Mounted Police would send in a single Mountie. All this contributed to a heroic legend that has endured.

Quickies

Did you know ...

- that since the early 19th century, over 800 Canadian police officers, jail and prison guards, and other law enforcement officers have died in the line of duty? The deaths have resulted from natural causes, accidents, and homicide.

What is the motto of the RCMP?

The official motto of the RCMP is *Maintiens le droit*, meaning "Uphold the Law." It is not, and never has been "We always get our man." That phrase can be traced back to an article that appeared in the Fort Benton, Montana, *Record* in April 1877. "The Mounted Police are worse than bloodhounds when they scent the track of a smuggler, and they fetch their man every time." Fort Benton was the main supply depot for the whiskey traders who were smuggling liquor into Canada.

What brought about the formation of the North West Mounted Police?

In 1870, Canada took over responsibility for Rupert's Land, the vast western domain of the Hudson's Bay Company. The land was being overrun by American whiskey traders who came north from Fort Benton and sold their illegal wares from whiskey posts like Fort Whoop Up. The liquor trade was having a devastating effect on the Native population, and was the cause of much violence and destruction. The North West Mounted Police Force was formed to put an end to the illegal liquor trade. Prime Minister John A. Macdonald also realized it was important for the Canadian government to establish sovereignty in the newly acquired West to head off any American ideas about annexation.

> **Quickies**
> *Did you know ...*
> • John A. Macdonald initially called the new force the North West Mounted Rifles? However, he was concerned that the Americans would be suspicious of a military presence in the Canadian West, so he changed *Rifles* to *Police*.

What was the "Great March" of the North West Mounted Police?

In the summer of 1874 the first troop of the NWMP, 300 men, made the long journey across the Canadian prairies to Fort Whoop Up, the most notorious of the American whiskey posts. In spite of the intense police training the men had undergone, they were poorly prepared for the march. It became an ordeal of hardship and endurance. The officers chose to blaze a new trail through unmapped territory instead of using a known trade route, and so got lost. The men suffered from the heat in their scarlet woolen tunics. Suitable drinking water was scarce, and the men went thirsty or were afflicted with diarrhea. Their Ontario-bred horses were not up to the rigours of the trail and began to die, which meant men had to pull supply wagons. Rain and a scarcity of fuel for cooking fires meant long periods without meals. When the men did eat, it was a monotonous diet of poorly made bread, salt bacon, and pancakes fried in axle grease. That the Mounties actually reached their objective was something of a miracle. The "Great March" is one of the enduring legends of the Mounties in Western Canada.

Who was Sam Steele?

Samuel Benfield Steele, born in Medonte Township, Upper Canada, in 1849, was the quintessential Mountie. He was one of the first men to sign up with the Force and he was in the Great March of 1874. Steele was involved in almost all of the significant events of 19th-century Western Canada, from the Northwest Rebellion to the construction of the Canadian Pacific Railway through the Rocky Mountains. He directed the manhunts for outlaws and killers, including the notorious renegades Almighty Voice and Charcoal. When the federal government threatened to disband the NWMP, Sam Steele was the Force's staunchest defender. Tall, handsome, ramrod-straight, and a man of action, Sam Steele was the personification of the romantic ideal of the Mountie.

Why was Sam Steele called "The Lion of the North"?

The Klondike Gold Rush of 1898 drew thousands of adventurers, most of them American, to the wilds of the Canadian Yukon. Dawson City was the El Dorado of the gold-rushers, and Skagway, Alaska, was the main port on one of the most well-travelled gold rush routes. Skagway was controlled by a criminal gang led by Jefferson Randolph "Soapy" Smith. Every gold-rusher passing through Skagway was at risk of being robbed, swindled, or murdered by the Smith gang. Sam Steele, now a NWMP superintendent, was sent to the Yukon to maintain law and order. He set up police posts on the passes leading to the Yukon interior. Steele's constables restricted entry to people who had enough provisions to last a year. They also turned away known members of the Soapy Smith gang, including Soapy himself. Steele also took measures to protect shipments of gold going out of the Yukon. Because of Steele's firm administration, the crime rate in the Yukon was relatively low during the gold rush, and Dawson City did not remotely resemble lawless Skagway. The order Steele brought to what could have been a chaotic situation helped to make the NWMP famous around the world. Soapy Smith was shot dead in Skagway in a confrontation with a vigilante mob.

> **Quickies**
> *Did you know ...*
> • Sam Steele served in the Boer War and in the First World War? He was knighted by King George V, and was made Knight Commander of the Most Distinguished Order of St. Michael and St. George, Companion of the Most Honourable Order of the Bath, and Member of the Royal Victorian Order. Sam Steele died in England on January 30, 1919, during the Spanish flu epidemic. He was buried in Winnipeg.

Who was the first North West Mounted Police constable to be murdered in the line of duty?

Constable Marmaduke Graburn, 19 years old and a Mountie for only six months, was shot to death on the night of November 17, 1879, near a Mounted Police post in what is now Saskatchewan. A Blood warrior named Star Child was accused of the murder, but was acquitted by a jury. The crime remains unsolved.

How did the Battle of the Little Bighorn cause a crisis for the NWMP?

On June 25, 1876, Sioux and Cheyenne warriors led by chiefs Sitting Bull and Crazy Horse wiped out the soldiers of the United States 7th Cavalry commanded by Lieutenant Colonel George A. Custer. Later, to escape

American vengeance, Sitting Bull led his people north to Canada, crossing the "Medicine Line" (international border) in 1877. He met Major James Morrow Walsh of the NWMP, and said that he and the Sioux with him wanted to live in the land of the Grandmother (Queen Victoria). Walsh was in a difficult spot. He did not have the manpower to force hundreds of battle-proven warriors to return to the United States, but he also knew he could not permit them to roam at will in Canada, especially since the Sioux were traditional enemies of the local Blackfoot. Also, the American army did not like the idea of Sitting Bull thumbing his nose at them from across the border, and put pressure on the Canadians to send him and his followers back. If the U.S. Army decided to cross the border and force the issue, a handful of Mounties wouldn't be able to stop them. The situation was potentially explosive.

Quickies

Did you know ...

• that in the autumn of 1876, with three American armies searching the plains for the Sioux and Cheyenne who had wiped out Custer's command, Americans were astonished at the activities of the NWMP? The Fort Benton, Montana, *Record* of October 13, 1876, reported, "The Mounted Police don't scare worth a cent. Parties of two and three men are scouting along the line looking for Sitting Bull."

Who was James Morrow Walsh?

Walsh was born in Prescott, Canada West (Ontario), in 1843. As a young man he had served in the militia and fought the Fenians. He was one of the first recruits to sign up with the NWMP. Because of his militia background he was made an inspector, with the honorary rank of major. He was with the Mounties who made the Great March, and had been very active in driving the American whiskey traders out of Canadian territory.

What role did the NWMP play in the Northwest Rebellion of 1885?

Although the Northwest Rebellion was ultimately crushed by a Canadian army at Batoche, the NWMP played a significant part in the events. The

Mounties fought skirmishes with the Métis and Natives, and were seen by the nervous white community as the first line of defence. They were instrumental in convincing some of the Native leaders not to join the Métis in armed insurrection.

How have the Mounties appeared as heroes in Hollywood movies?

The American movie industry never misses a chance to cash in on a romantic image or a melodramatic story. The exotic (to Americans) appeal of the Mountie as the tough, resourceful lawman who "always gets his man" was irresistible to American filmmakers as far back as the era of silent movies. Canadian Mounties rode across the silver screen in pursuit of renegade Indians, treacherous "half-breeds," and cunning outlaws in dozens of feature films and serials. None of them were historically accurate. An Alan Ladd movie had mountains in Saskatchewan. A James Stewart movie had a Mountie telling the people of Dawson City they should elect a town sheriff. But for all these maddening errors, Hollywood has nonetheless helped to perpetuate the image of the Mountie as a hero.

Mounties Killed in the Northwest Rebellion

Duck Lake
- Constable Thomas J. Gibson
- Constable George K. Garrett
- Constable George P. Arnold

Fort Pitt
- Constable David L. Cowan

Cut Knife Hill
- Corporal Ralph B. Sleigh
- Corporal William H.T. Lowry
- Constable Patrick Burke

Battleford
- Constable Frank O. Elliott

Quickies
Did you know ...
- that compared to the many American soldiers who were killed in "Indian wars" during the years of the Wild West, only a handful of Mounties were slain by Natives? Sergeant Colin Colebrook was killed trying to arrest the Cree Almighty Voice. Constable John R. Kerr and Corporal Charles Sterling Hockin were killed when a posse tried to flush Almighty Voice and two companions out of a poplar bluff. Sergeant William Brock Wilde was killed by the Blood Warrior, Charcoal.

Twenty Movie Stars Who Played Mounties on Film

- Tom Mix — *The Cyclone*, 1920
- Lewis Stone — *River's End*, 1920
- Eugene O'Brien — *Channing of the Northwest*, 1922
- Charles Byer — *Red Riders of Canada*, 1928
- James Hall — *Dangerous Dan McGrew*, 1930
- Buck Jones — *McKenna of the Mounted*, 1932
- Kermit Maynard — *Code of the Mounted*, 1935
- Nelson Eddie — *Rose Marie*, 1936
- Buster Brown — *Renfrew of the Royal Mounted*, 1937
- Randolph Scott — *Susannah of the Mounties*, 1939
- Robert Preston — *Northwest Mounted Police*, 1940
- James Newill — *Murder on the Yukon*, 1940
- Bob Steele — *Northwest Trail*, 1946
- Wendell Corey — *The Wild North*, 1951
- Bill Henry — *Canadian Mounties Versus the Atomic Invaders*, 1953
- Tyrone Power, —*Pony Soldier*, 1952
- Alan Ladd — *Saskatchewan*, 1954
- Robert Ryan — *The Canadians*, 1961
- Donald Sutherland — *Alien Thunder* (also titled *Dan Candy's Law*), 1974
- Lee Marvin — *Death Hunt*, 1981

How did Isaac Decker go to a hero's death?

In 1909, Isaac Decker was a retired British Columbia provincial policeman who, in his younger days, had gained fame for the single-handed capture of American gunfighter and killer Frank Spence. After a train robbery took place on June 21, 1909, Decker was asked to come out of retirement just long enough to help apprehend the gang responsible. Decker confronted two of the suspects, Bill and Dave Haney, in the town of Ashcroft. There was a shootout. Decker killed Dave Haney, but Bill Haney killed Decker with a shotgun blast. Bill Haney fled to the United States and was never brought back to Canada to face charges for Decker's murder.

Who was Canada's "Great Detective"?

James Wilson Murray, originally from Scotland, became a detective for the province of Ontario in 1875 and held the position almost until the time of his death in 1906. Murray was Canada's own Sherlock Holmes. He was one of the first to use scientific methods in crime investigation. Murray solved hundreds of crimes, including a multi-million-dollar counterfeiting operation. Perhaps his most famous case was the murder of Frederick

Benwell. Murray tracked down the killer, John Reginald Birchall, who was subsequently hanged.

What major obstacle did Montreal police detective Georges Farah-Lajoie face in 1922?

Detective Farah-Lajoie had the job of tracking down the killer of Raoul Delorme, whose bullet-riddled body had been found on a Montreal street corner. It was important that the murderer be found quickly, because Raoul was the brother of Father Adelard Delorme, a high-profile priest. In Quebec at that time, members of the Roman Catholic clergy were powerful figures, socially and politically. If murder was shocking, the murder of a person related to a priest was doubly so. Detective Farah-Lajoie's task became especially difficult when all of the evidence pointed to Father Delorme as the killer. At first his superiors wanted him to drop any notions that the priest was the killer, but Farah-Lajoie could not ignore the evidence. When the news broke, the province of Quebec was shaken to the very core. Farah-Lajoie received death threats.

Quickies
Did you know ...
- John Wilson Murray wrote a book about his most famous cases, *Memoirs of a Great Detective*? Unfortunately, he had a tendency to embellish his stories, which somewhat limits the book's value as a historical source.

The newspapers called him anti-clerical and a pagan. His children were abused at school. His wife's priest (Farah-Lajoie was not Catholic) pleaded with her to convince her husband to stop investigating Father Delorme. The priest had friends in high places, and he threatened to use his connections to make trouble for the detective. But in spite of all this, Farah-Lajoie pressed on with his investigation. The notorious Delorme case went through four trials. In spite of overwhelming evidence against Father Delorme, the juries could not bring themselves to convict a priest. Father Delorme was free to go. The Catholic Church assigned him to a posting under a different name. Detective Farah-Lajoie, who at the time was probably Montreal's best homicide detective, eventually became a private investigator.

How did the murder of a policeman bring about the end of the Boyd Gang?

For some time the bank-robbing exploits of Edwin Alonzo Boyd and his partners Lennie Jackson, Steve Suchan, and Willie "The Clown" Jackson (no relation to Lennie) had practically made them Canadian folk heroes. Then, on March 6, 1952, Detective Sergeant Edmund Tong, an officer who was himself something of a legend in Toronto, approached a car occupied by Suchan and Lennie Jackson. Without warning Suchan pulled a gun and shot Tong in the stomach. Suchan also wounded Tong's partner, Sergeant Roy Perry. On March 23, Tong died. With the shooting of Tong, public opinion turned against the Boyd gang. All of the members were soon rounded up. Suchan and Lennie Jackson were hanged for the policeman's murder.

larger-
than-life legends

How did a pirate become a Newfoundland folk hero?

Peter Easton, the "Pirate Admiral of Newfoundland" was a captain in Queen Elizabeth I's navy who turned pirate when King James I made peace with Spain and mothballed the English fleet. In 1611, Easton built a fort at present-day Harbour Grace, Newfoundland, and used it as a base from which to raid the Spanish Main to the south. Easton plundered the Newfoundland fisheries for supplies, and many a Newfoundland fisherman happily joined Easton's pirate crews. Easton was probably one of the most successful pirates in history, getting away with loot that today would amount to millions of dollars. Easton became a legendary folk hero in Newfoundland. A community was named after his ship, the *Happy Adventure*, and an islet now called Eastern Rock was originally called Easton's Rock.

Quickies

Did you know ...

- when Easton returned from one of his marauds against the Spanish, he found his fort at Harbour Grace in the hands of French Basques? There was a battle in which Easton defeated the Basques, but 47 of his pirates were killed. They were buried at a place that is still called the Pirates' Graveyard. It is the only known pirate burial ground in North America.

Why were Peter Kerrivan and his followers called "Masterless Men"?

In the early days of the Newfoundland fisheries, life for the fishermen and the shore workers who cleaned and cured the fish was extremely hard. They worked in almost slave-like conditions for next to nothing. Many of them fled inland to take their chances living life in the wild. This was against the law, as they were all bound to their masters, the merchants who owned the fishing fleets. Parties of armed men would be sent out to hunt down these "masterless men" and bring them back to St. John's for hanging. The Masterless Men found a leader in Peter Kerrivan, a wily character who was always able to give the posses the slip. Kerrivan may well have been one of North America's first outlaw heroes.

Who was the "White Savage"?

"White savage," "beast in human form," and "good for nothin' dog" were just a few of the names the Americans had for frontiersman Simon Girty during the Revolutionary War and for generations after. Girty was captured by Natives as a boy and lived among them for years, learning their languages and adapting to their customs. Soon after the war broke out, Girty became an agent for the British Indian Department, and worked as an interpreter and spy. He also accompanied Britain's Native allies in raids against American frontier settlements. The Americans told grossly exaggerated tales of Girty's bloodthirsty cruelty, and made him one of the most vilified characters in American history. After the British defeat, Girty moved to a farm near Malden in Upper Canada, but continued to assist his Native friends to resist American expansion. He died in his Canadian home in 1818 and has been honoured with a historic plaque. In Canada, Girty is considered a Loyalist hero and a champion of the Native cause.

> **Quickies**
> *Did you know ...*
> - Simon Girty has appeared as a villain in several American works of fiction, including Stephen Vincent Benet's classic *The Devil and Daniel Webster*? In the 1936 film *Daniel Boone,* arch villain Simon Girty was portrayed by horror star John Carradine, who wore a skunk-skin cap for the role. However, Simon Girty was the model for the heroic if incorrigible Sampson Gattrie in John Richardson's novel *The Canadian Brothers.*

Who was the real Big Joe Mufferaw?

The legendary Big Joe Mufferaw of the Ottawa Valley was in fact Joseph Montferrand, the Montreal-born hero of Quebec loggers. As a youth Montferrand was a voyageur for the Hudson's Bay Company, but in 1827 he went to work in the woods. He stood six-foot-four, was powerfully built, and it was said that as a lad of 16, he had knocked out a Royal Navy boxing champion in a bout in Quebec City. Montferrand was easy-going and generous by nature, but in the brawling timber camps and rugged communities of the Ottawa Valley, he was a force to be reckoned with, especially in the battles between the French

Canadians and Irish hoodlums known as Shiners. Montferrand allegedly single-handedly routed a gang of Shiners when they thought they had him trapped on the bridge between Hull and Bytown. He also walloped the Shiner's main tough guy, Big Martin Hennesy, in a celebrated saloon fight. Montferrand allegedly could leap into the air and leave the heel marks of his logging boots in a saloon ceiling. After his death in 1864, Montferrand was immortalized in song and story. His admirers have included Sir Wilfrid Laurier, author of a biography, and Stompin' Tom Connors, who wrote the ballad *Big Joe Mufferaw.*

Who was the Cape Breton Giant?

Giant Angus McAskill was born in Scotland in 1825 but grew up (literally) in St. Ann's, Cape Breton. McAskill was a normal sized baby, but he grew to an adult height of seven feet, nine inches. He weighed 425 pounds and had a girth of 80 inches, the largest known on a non-obese man. Initially McAskill was a farmer and a fisherman, but due to his size and incredible physical strength he went on the road with a circus. He returned to Cape Breton with a small fortune and opened a general store which he ran until his sudden death in 1863 at the age of 38. There are many stories about McAskill's tremendous feats of strength and of his acts of kindness and generosity. Angus McAskill was once listed in the *Guinness Book of Records* as the world's biggest non-pathological giant. He is still regarded as a folk hero in Cape Breton. His grave can still be seen at Englishtown, Cape Breton, near a small museum that displays some of his personal belongings.

What was the connection between a 19th-century Polish rebellion and a popular CBC Radio talk show host?

In 1830, Casimir Gzowski, a Polish aristocrat, participated in a revolt against Russia. The Russian army crushed the insurrection, and Gzowski was wounded in the fighting. After his release from prison, Gzowski eventually made his way to Canada. He was a trained military engineer, and he earned fame, fortune, and honours for being one of the builders of the Grand Trunk Railway. One of his greatest engineering accomplishments was the construction of the international bridge at Niagara Falls. The former hero of the Polish rebellion was the great-grandfather of the late host of CBC's *Morningside* radio show, Peter Gzowski.

Quickies
Did you know ...
- that according to one of the many stories told about Giant McAskill, he once carried a sick man on his back 25 miles through a snowstorm without once setting him down, in order to get the man to a doctor?

Who said, "Boys, if there is shooting in Kootenay, there will be hanging in Kootenay!"?

Judge Matthew Begbie used that warning to quell an unruly gang of armed miners who were about to riot in the streets of Wild Horse Creek during the Kootenay Gold Rush. In 1858, the British government sent Begbie to the wilds of British Columbia to impose the rule of law. Begbie was flamboyant, autocratic, and determined that the violence and anarchy that had made the gold camps of California notorious would not be repeated in British Columbia. Many of the gold hunters were American adventurers who hated all things British, including Judge Begbie. But thanks to Begbie's firm but fair administration of justice, law and order prevailed in British Columbia. Begbie became Chief Justice of British Columbia in 1866 and held the post until his death in 1894. He was granted a knighthood by Queen Victoria.

Why is Alexander Milton Ross, a white doctor, honoured during Black History Month?

A native of Belleville, Canada West (Ontario), Dr. Ross was a physician and a well-known naturalist and ornithologist who wrote for the *Evening Post* in New York. He was also a dedicated abolitionist. On several occasions Dr. Ross travelled through the southern States, supposedly to study birds and nature. This gave him a reason to be out in the fields where he had close contact with slaves. He would tell them about the Underground Railroad, and provide them with money, maps, compasses, knives, and even pistols. Sometimes he personally guided them across the border at Niagara Falls and Windsor. This was extremely dangerous work, and on at least one occasion Dr. Ross came close to being lynched by angry southerners who suspected him of helping runaway slaves.

Who was Klondike Joe Boyle?

Born in Toronto in 1867, Joseph W. Boyle lived an adventurous life worthy of a Hollywood movie. He was a sailor, an entrepreneur, a boxer, a gold hunter, a secret agent, and the confidant of royalty. He

had already packed a lifetime of exotic experience into his 30 years when he joined the Klondike Gold Rush in 1897. Boyle made a fortune by using hydraulic methods to extract gold. In 1904–05 Boyle financed a Yukon hockey team, the Wanderers, which unsuccessfully challenged the Ottawa Silver Seven for the Stanley Cup. In the First World War, Boyle recruited and equipped a 50-man machine-gun company. His unit was incorporated into the Canadian army. In 1917 Boyle went to Russia to help organize the country's chaotic railway system. In the midst of the Russian Revolution, Boyle managed to become a national hero to Romania by rescuing 50 high-ranking Romanians as well as some important documents. It was even rumoured that Boyle had a romantic affair with Romania's Queen Marie. Boyle was decorated by the governments of Great Britain, France, Romania, and Russia. He died in 1923 and is buried in Woodstock, Ontario.

Why is "Wild Goose Jack" a hero to conservationists?

John Thomas "Jack" Miner was born in Ohio but moved with his family to Essex County, Ontario, as a boy. In his youth, Miner was an avid hunter and trapper, but had a change of heart after his brother was killed in a hunting accident. Miner began to take an interest in nature, particularly birds and migration. In 1904 he created a pond on his farm with a few clipped, tame Canada geese that he hoped would attract wild geese. It took a few years, but eventually thousands of wild geese were attracted to Miner's homemade sanctuary, the first of its kind in North America. Miner was the first to start banding ducks and geese in order to unlock the mysteries of migration routes. A direct result of his studies was the 1917 Migratory Bird Treaty between Canada and the United States. Right up until his death in 1944, Wild Goose Jack lectured on the importance of conservation. In 1943, King George VI presented him with the Order of the British Empire (OBE).

Why is Sir Wilfred Grenfell fondly remembered in Newfoundland and Labrador?

Wilfred Grenfell was an English medical missionary who founded the Grenfell Mission and opened the first hospital at Battle Harbour in 1893. From his headquarters in St. Anthony, Newfoundland, Grenfell cruised the coasts of Newfoundland and Labrador bringing medical assistance to people who might otherwise never see a doctor. The International Grenfell Association, which grew from the mission, still funds scholarships for medical training. Grenfell was knighted for his work, and in 1911 received the Murchison Prize from the Royal Geographic Society. In 1997 he was inducted into the Canadian Medical Hall of Fame. There is a statue of Grenfell in St. Anthony, and his house there is now a museum.

Why were the Canadian bush pilots considered larger-than-life heroes?

In the early years of aviation, the bush pilots were as highly romanticized as the cowboys of an earlier era had been. They were seen as rugged individualists who had something most people could only dream of, the freedom of the skies. Because of northern geography, weather conditions, and the great distances between departure points and destinations, bush flying was much more dangerous than conventional flying. It took above average skill and nerve for a pilot to master bush flying, which is probably why so many of the first bush pilots were former First World War fighter pilots. The bush pilots were a vital lifeline between remote northern communities and the outside world. The trip to an isolated location that once took many days by canoe or dogsled, took just a few hours by plane. Bush pilots carried passengers, mail, and every sort of cargo. They airlifted sick and injured people to city hospitals. In 1932, Wilfrid "Wop" May, perhaps the most famous of the Canadian bush pilots, participated in the hunt for the killer known as the Mad Trapper of Rat River, and was instrumental in helping the RCMP track the outlaw down.

Who was the first bush pilot to fly the Barren Lands of the Northwest Territories?

Clennell Haggerston "Punch" Dickins of Portage la Prairie, Manitoba, earned the Distinguished Flying Cross in the First World War for shooting down seven enemy planes. After the war, Punch Dickins became one of the greatest pioneers in Canadian aviation. He was a test pilot for the Royal Canadian Air Force, he flew forestry patrols, and he conducted photographic surveys for the government. In August 1928, Dickins made an unprecedented 12-day flight over the Barren Lands that totalled more than 4,000 miles. He flew from Chesterfield Inlet on Hudson Bay to the western shore of Lake Athabasca in Saskatchewan. This was nearly all uncharted territory, and the proximity of the North Magnetic Pole made navigation by compass impossible. Punch Dickins's flight was a landmark event in bush flying. For this and other achievements in aviation, Punch was made an Officer of the British Empire and an Officer of the Order of Canada.

What was "The Canadian Caper"?

On November 5, 1979, Islamic militants stormed the American embassy in Tehran, Iran, and took more than 70 people hostage. Six Americans who were not in the embassy at the time were secretly sheltered by Canadian ambassador Ken Taylor and his wife Pat, and Canadian immigration official John Sheardown and his wife Zena. The weeks that followed were tense as the Iranians searched for the missing Americans. In small groups, Canadian embassy staff quietly left the country. Finally, on January 27, 1980, the six Americans passed through Tehran airport using Canadian passports and escaped. Taylor then closed down the Canadian embassy and returned to Canada. As the architect of the "Canadian Caper," Taylor became an instant hero in Canada and the United States. He was made an Officer of the Order of Canada and was awarded a Congressional gold medal by the government of the United States.

valiant women

How did an aristocratic French girl become a Canadian Robinson Crusoe?

In 1642, while en route to founding a colony in New France, Jean Francois de la Rocque de Roberval, a rather unscrupulous character, discovered that his niece Marguerite was romantically involved with a common sailor. As punishment for this shame on his family honour, Roberval marooned Marguerite, her lover, and a female servant on an uninhabited island (probably Fogo Island) off the coast of Newfoundland. The three endured extreme hardships. The young man and the servant died, as did a baby to whom Marguerite had given birth. Marguerite endured two and a half years of privation and extreme loneliness before she was finally rescued by fishermen. Back in France, Marguerite was "received with great honour by all the women." She told her story to André Thévet, one of the earliest chroniclers of New France. Marguerite's determined struggle to survive made her one of colonial Canada's first heroes.

Why was Marie Jacqueline de la Tour called "a musketeer in petticoats"?

Marie was the wife of Charles de Saint-Étienne de La Tour, a fur trader who was involved in a vicious feud over control of the French colony of Acadia. His headquarters, Fort La Tour, was at the site of present-day Saint John, New Brunswick. Across the Bay of Fundy was Port Royal (now Annapolis Royal, Nova Scotia), commanded by Charles de Menou d'Aulnay. La Tour and d'Aulnay each considered Acadia to be his own turf, and was determined to drive the other out. The feud lasted for several years, and Marie's life with La Tour was one of adventure and intrigue. Early in 1647, La Tour left Marie in charge of the fort while he went to the English settlement of Boston to get supplies. Deserters from Fort La Tour went to Port Royal and told d'Aulnay that La Tour was away. Seizing the opportunity, d'Aulnay crossed the bay with two shiploads of men and, on April 12, 1645, he attacked Fort La Tour.

Marie took command of the defence, and for three days the "musketeer in petticoats" and her 45 men held the attackers at bay. They killed 20 of d'Aulnay's men and sank one of his ships. Then a traitor in the fort helped d'Aulnay get inside. After a sharp hand-to-hand fight, Marie surrendered on d'Aulnay's promise that the lives of her men would be spared. D'Aulnay promptly broke that promise, and had all of the men hanged. Three weeks later Marie died, quite possibly by poisoning, though some people claimed it was from a broken heart.

Quickies

Did you know ...

- that a few years after his victory at Fort La Tour, d'Aulnay drowned in the Bay of Fundy? Charles de La Tour married his widow and became the official lieutenant-governor of Acadia.

Who was "The Heroine of Vercheres"?

On October 22, 1692, 14-year-old Madeleine Jarret Tarieu was working in a vegetable garden about 200 paces from the gate of Fort Verchères, a wooden stockade on her father's seigneury. In the summer of 1691, Madeleine's brother and two brothers-in-law had been killed in Iroquois raids. But the summer of 1692 had been so quiet, that when October came and there had been no attacks, her father decided it would be safe for him to travel to Quebec City on business, while Madeleine's mother went to Montreal to buy supplies. Madeleine was left in charge of Verchères, with just one elderly soldier for protection. Suddenly 40 or 50 Iroquois warriors swept out of the forest. They captured about 20 of the settlers who had been working in the fields. Madeleine ran for the gate, with a warrior in pursuit. He caught hold of her scarf, but she tore it off and got away. She ran through the gate crying, "To arms! To arms!" as she slammed it shut.

Most of the people in the stockade were women and children. Madeleine took command. She fired the small cannon, knowing it would be heard in other settlements. She put on a soldier's hat and let herself be seen at the wall, gesturing, shouting, and giving the impression that the fort was full of soldiers. After dark, when the settlers' cattle came to the gate, Madeleine did not open up to allow them in, knowing there could be Iroquois hiding among them. The following day the Iroquois fled before a relief party of 100 soldiers and 50 Native allies. All but two of the captured settlers were freed. The Heroine of Verchères became a Canadian symbol of courage and determination. Today, in the village of Verchères a statue of Madeleine overlooks the St. Lawrence River.

> **Quickies**
> *Did you know ...*
> * that years later, Madeleine wrote a letter to the Comtesse de Maurepas in which she gave a rather embellished account of her defence of the fort? The Comtesse passed the story on to King Louis XIV, who was so impressed that he arranged for Madeleine to receive her late father's pension.

How did a young Chipewyan woman almost single-handedly stop a war?

In 1714, Thanadelthur of the Chipewyan nation escaped captivity among the rival Cree and fled to the Hudson's Bay Company post of York Factory. She spoke Chipewyan and Cree, and became an interpreter for Governor James Knight. Warfare between the two tribes was hurting the fur trade, so Knight sent out a diplomatic mission to convince the Chipewyan to come to York Factory and make peace with the Cree. A Company man named William Stuart was officially in command of the mission, but Thanadelthur soon proved to be its driving force. Under extremely difficult conditions she convinced the Chipewyan to attend the meeting. Then she literally browbeat the two sides into accepting a peace treaty. She was eloquent and she was hot tempered, but she got the job done. Stuart wrote in a letter, "She made them all stand in fear of her. She scolded some and pushing of others ... and forced them to ye peace." Knight wrote of Thanadelthur, "Indeed she has a Devillish Spirit and I believe if there were but 50 of her Country Men of the Same Carriage and Resolution they

> **Quickies**
> *Did you know ...*
> * that during the Second World War, a dramatic recruiting poster showing a determined-looking Madeleine wearing her soldier's hat and holding a musket was used to encourage Canadian women to join the women's auxiliary branches of the armed forces?

would drive all the (Southern) Indians of America out of there [*sic*] Country." Sadly, in January of 1717, Thanadelthur fell ill and died. She was probably no more than 20 years old. Knight wrote in his journal, "I am almost ready to break my heart."

Why was the wife of the commander of Fortress Louisbourg called *La Bombardiere*?

Augustine de Boschenry de Droucour was in command of Fortress Louisbourg on Cape Breton Island when it was besieged by a British army under Major General Jeffrey Amherst and Brigadier General James Wolfe in 1758. As British cannonballs rained down on the town, morale among soldiers and citizens alike was low. To raise the people's spirits, the commander's wife, Madame Droucour, would go to the ramparts everyday and fire three of the big guns in the name of the king. The people all cheered this show of defiance by *La Bombardiere*. Nonetheless, Louisbourg was eventually captured.

Why was Mrs. Bowman a Loyalist heroine?

Quickies

Did you know ...

- that just because they were at war did not mean the opposing commanders could not observe social niceties? General Amherst sent a basket of pineapples into the beleaguered fortress for Madame Droucour. *La Bombardiere* and her husband responded to this display of gallantry by sending some butter and champagne to Amherst, and a box of sweetmeats to Wolfe.

Jacob Bowman was a farmer in the colony of New York. When the American Revolution broke out, he and his 16-year-old son were dragged off to prison on suspicion of being Tories. A Patriot gang stripped his house of everything, including clothing and bedding. Jacob's wife, known only as Mrs. Bowman, was expecting, and was left with nothing but a single blanket on which to deliver her baby. Her six small children were even robbed of their coats and shoes. The family would have perished if not for some friendly Natives who helped them through the hard winter and then escorted them to Fort George, Niagara. By now, Mrs. Bowman's second-oldest son was 13, so she gave him permission to join Butler's Rangers. His nine-year-old brother went along as a fifer. Not until the war ended in 1783 did Mrs. Bowman see her husband and oldest son again, after they had endured eight years of hell in prison. Like most Loyalists, the Bowmans were not compensated by the new American government for their losses or privations. Mrs. Bowman was seen as a heroic representative of the plight of Loyalist women who endured persecution and started life anew in Canada.

Who was "Miss Molly"?

Molly Brant was the sister of the great Mohawk leader Joseph Brant. She was also the wife (according to Native customs) of Sir William Johnson, the Superintendent of Indian Affairs for the colony of New York, until his sudden death in 1774. Miss Molly, as many people called her, was vital to Sir William in his work because she was an expert interpreter and as a Matron of the Mohawk nation she had prestige and influence. This made her very important to the British when the Revolutionary War broke out in 1776. The American rebels promised the tribes of the Iroquois Confederacy that if the warriors fought on their side, they could keep their lands when the war was over. Joseph and Molly Brant did not trust the Americans, and convinced most of the tribes to fight for the king. The Brants were proven correct when, after the war, the Americans took the lands of their Oneida and Tuscarora allies. During the war Molly Brant was invaluable to the British for her work as an interpreter, a spy, and an emissary to the tribes. One British officer wrote that "Miss Molly Brant's influence ... is far superior to that of all their chiefs put together."

What was remarkable about Louis Riel's grandmother?

Quite a lot was remarkable about the adventurous, 95-year-long life of Marie-Anne Gaboury Lagemodiere. She was born in Trois-Rivières,

Quebec, in 1780, and from age 12 to 26 she worked in domestic service. Then she married Jean-Baptiste Lagemodiere, an independent fur trader who had just returned from Rupert's Land. Right after the marriage, Lagemodiere announced he was returning to Rupert's Land with a group of voyageurs. Marie-Anne insisted that she was going, too, and when the voyageurs set off in early June 1806, Marie-Anne was in one of the big freight canoes. From that moment on her life changed. She made the long journey from Montreal to the lakehead of Lake Superior, and then continued on with Jean-Baptiste to the junction of the Red and Assiniboine rivers at the site of Winnipeg. She was the first white woman on the prairies, and her sons and daughters were the first white children born on the prairies. Marie-Anne experienced all the hardships of being a hunter-trapper's wife in a frontier environment, and then some. She was threatened by a Native woman who had previously been Jean-Baptiste's "country wife," and she once had to rescue her infant son when he was kidnapped by another woman. They travelled throughout Rupert's Land, but were back in the Red River country in time to witness the trouble involving the ill-fated Selkirk settlement. Jean-Baptiste was imprisoned for a time in the North West Company's post at Fort William for carrying Hudson's Bay Company dispatches to Montreal. While he was gone, Marie-Anne and the children lived with a band of Ojibwa. Lord Selkirk rewarded Jean-Baptiste by giving him a large land grant on the east bank of the Red River. The Lagemodieres built a large house and lived there for many years. It was there, in 1822, that Marie-Anne's daughter Julie was born in 1822. She in turn would be the mother of Louis Riel.

Who was "the Laura Secord of Gananoque"?

Elizabeth Barnett was an American-born schoolteacher who had moved to Gananoque on the St. Lawrence River and become a Canadian citizen. In February of 1838, while visiting relatives on the American side, she heard of a planned invasion of Canada by men who called themselves Patriots. They were going to seize the undefended town of Gananoque, and then with the help of traitors, capture Kingston and Fort Henry. Thus, they would control Upper Canada and would "liberate" the Canadians from the evil British. Elizabeth also learned that Bill Johnston, the notorious Pirate of the Thousand Islands, was one of the leaders of the invasion force. Pretending to be ill, she cut her visit short. She drove 10 miles across the frozen-over, windswept St. Lawrence River in a one-horse cutter to deliver the warning. The following day about 2,000 Patriots marched from French Creek, New York, to Hickory Island, which was to be the jumping off place for the surprise attack on Gananoque. They learned to their own surprise that Gananoque was packed with soldiers and militia who were dug in and waiting for them. Deeming discretion the better part of valour, the Patriots all went home. Oddly enough, Elizabeth Barnett's story is little known, and even those who do appreciate the importance of what she did, label her with another heroine's name, "the Laura Secord of Gananoque."

Who was the Heroine of Long Point?

Abigail Becker, a big, strong woman who stood six-foot-two, was the wife of a trapper and fisherman who lived on Long Point, a peninsula jutting from the Canadian shore into the eastern end of Lake Erie. The waters around Long Point were deadly to shipping because of the many shifting sandbars. Abigail gained international fame for her heroic rescues of men from several shipwrecks, most notably that of the schooner *Conductor* in November of 1854. Even though she couldn't

---

Quickies

Did you know ...

- poet Amanda T. Jones wrote a ballad about Abigail Becker called, "A Heroine of '54" which was used in a textbook, *The Ontario High School Reader*? It goes, in part:

    O Mother Becker, seas are dread
    Their treacherous paths are deep and blind
    But widows soon may mourn their dead
    If thou art slow to find

swim, Abigail braved the cold, rough water to save the *Conductor's* captain and seven crewmen. For this courageous deed, Abigail received a letter of commendation from Queen Victoria, a letter of congratulations from the governor general of Canada, and was awarded a gold medal by the Benevolent Life Saving Association of New York. She was the guest of honour at a banquet in Buffalo where she was presented with a purse of $550. In 1860 she was visited by the Prince of Wales (later King Edward VII). Abigail Becker is remembered in the lore of Great Lakes navigation as the Angel of Long Point.

What was Dr. James Miranda Barry's great secret?

In 1857, British army surgeon James Miranda Barry, one of the most distinguished doctors of his time, came to Canada to be the inspector general of hospitals and barracks. Nobody knew that the doctor, in his mid-sixties, was really a woman who had been baptized Margaret Bulkley. Years earlier she had disguised herself as a man so she could attend medical school, which in those days was forbidden to women. Dr. Barry was a friend to common soldiers wherever he (she) was posted in the British Empire because he fought for their right to have things like a healthy diet, safe drinking water, clean barracks and bedding, and even private quarters for married soldiers. The first thing he did upon arrival in Quebec City was get rid of the open sewers that ran through the military compound. Dr. Barry was in Canada for only two years, but his work saved the lives of many soldiers. Not until Dr. Barry died in London in 1865 was it discovered that "he" was a woman. The army and the medical association tried to keep the matter hushed up.

Quickies

Did you know ...

- Dr. James Miranda Barry, not surprisingly, championed the cause of decent medical care for women, particularly pregnant women? He (she) studied midwifery and gynecology — fields that many physicians ignored — and was the first British surgeon to successfully perform a Caesarean section.

Who was Mary Ann Shadd?

Mary Ann Shadd was a free-born Black American teacher, journalist, and abolitionist who moved to Canada West (Ontario) in 1851 following the American government's passage of the Fugitive Slave Act, which was a threat to every Black person in the United States, whether free or in servitude. She established schools for escaped slaves and their children who made it to Canada via the Underground Railroad. Against all odds she founded a publication, *The Provincial Freeman,* which was considered the best abolitionist newspaper of the time. She thus became the first Black female editor and publisher of a newspaper in North America. Her articles attacked not only slavery, but also the stereotyping of Black people being unsophisticated and childlike, and always in need of help from white people. At the same time, she disagreed with Black leaders in Canada who argued that Blacks should live in segregated communities. Mary Ann Shadd believed in integration. After the Civil War she returned to the United States and became the first woman to graduate from Howard Law School. She died in Washington, D.C., in 1893.

Quickies
Did you know ...
- Mary Ann Shadd had to deal with gender prejudice as well as racial bigotry? When subscribers to *The Provincial Freeman* learned that the newspaper's editor was a woman, many of them threatened to cancel their subscriptions. To save the paper, she got permission from Reverend William P. Newman, an influential Black clergyman, to use his name as a "front." She didn't like having to resort to such a deception, but felt *The Provincial Freeman's* message was more important than her pride.

What New Brunswick farm girl became a top Civil War spy?

Sarah Emma Edmonds ran away from her father's New Brunswick farm to escape an arranged marriage. She first disguised herself as a man to get a job as a travelling bible salesman. She was in Flint, Michigan, when the Civil War broke out. Sarah joined the Union Army as a male nurse named Frank Thompson. Soon Frank Thompson was also employed as a dispatch courier. But Frank Thompson's greatest contribution to the military was as a spy. While no one in the Union army suspected that the brave young soldier was a woman, Frank Thompson made numerous forays behind Confederate lines to study their gun emplacements and fortifications and even to steal documents. Every mission was fraught with peril, and every one was successful, because Frank Thompson was a master of disguises. When Frank's superiors finally decided that it was getting too dangerous to send him into enemy territory, they instead used him to infiltrate a Confederate spy operation behind their own lines. Not until 1882, 17 years after the end of the war, did Sara reveal that she was Frank Thompson.

How did Clara Brett Martin challenge the Law Society of Ontario?

Quickies

Did you know ...

- that before Clara Brett Martin's heroic struggle to be allowed to study law, women were barred not only from being lawyers; they were also forbidden to be magistrates, coroners, jurors, legislators, or voters? Anti-suffrage hardliners in the Ontario Law Society put up a stiff fight to keep Clara out, because they were afraid that if women became lawyers, they would soon be challenging the laws that denied them the right to vote.

In 1891, 17-year-old Clara Brett Martin, an honours graduate of Toronto's Trinity College, applied for admission to study law at the Law Society of Upper Canada. She was refused on the grounds that only "persons" could study law, and women were not recognized as persons. Clara then petitioned to be admitted as a student-at-law, with the support of the Dominion Women's Enfranchisement Association and a few members of the Ontario Legislature. In 1892, a bill was passed that permitted the Law Society to admit women to study law. However, it limited women lawyers to being solicitors. They could not

be barristers. That meant they could have clients, but could not represent them in court. This was a compromise intended to appease the suffrage movement. Clara Brett Martin continued to press for the right to be a full barrister. Among her supporters were Emily Stowe, Lady Aberdeen, and Ontario Premier Sir Oliver Mowat. Clara won her fight in 1897 when she became the first woman admitted to the bar in Canada, and in the British Empire.

Quickies
Did you know ...
- a bronze bust of Agnes MacPhail was installed in the House of Commons after her death in 1954? Former prime minister John Diefenbaker once said that Canada had produced five great politicians, and Agnes MacPhail was one of them.

Who was Canada's first woman member of Parliament?

In 1921, a small political party called the United Farmers of Ontario chose Agnes MacPhail as its candidate for the constituency of South-East Grey (later Grey Bruce). She was the only one of four women running in that year's federal election to win a seat in Parliament, making her Canada's first female MP. Born on a farm in Grey County in 1890, Agnes had been a schoolteacher, but had never been involved in the suffrage movement. However, she was strong-minded and a champion for the cause of social reform. In an age when most Canadians, including many women, considered politics a man's world, Agnes MacPhail was a pioneer. She fought for such reforms as crop failure insurance for farmers, unemployment insurance, family allowance, old age pensions, and prison reform. She was a pacifist who spoke against war even when it was unpopular to do so. Agnes held her federal seat until 1940, when a blizzard on election day prevented many of her rural constituents from voting. She turned to provincial politics, and in 1943 became one of the first two women to serve in the Ontario legislature.

How did an American-born socialite become "First Lady of the Yukon"?

Martha Black (*nee* Munger) was the daughter of well-to-do parents in Chicago. She was the socialite wife of railway heir Will Purdy when the Klondike Gold Rush swept America. Martha got caught up in the adventure, even though her husband didn't. She travelled north with the stampeders and fell in love with the Yukon. She not only struck gold, but also established businesses that enabled her to put down roots in the North. She married a lawyer named George Black, who was eventually made commissioner of the Yukon Territory. As the Yukon's official First Lady, Martha became a Canadian citizen. George Black became a federal member of Parliament and was re-elected three times. In 1935, when illness forced George to temporarily retire from politics, Martha ran in his place and won the election, becoming Canada's second female member of Parliament. She was almost 70 years old at the time. In 1949, she was presented with the Order of the British Empire.

Individual Accomplishments of the Famous Five

- Nellie McClung — acclaimed novelist, member of the Legislative Assembly of Alberta, first woman member of the Canadian Broadcasting Corporation's Board of Governors.
- Emily Murphy — renowned journalist, first woman magistrate in Canada.
- Henrietta Muir Edwards — co-founder of the National Council for Women and the Victorian Order of Nurses.
- Irene Parlby — first woman cabinet minister in Alberta, president of the United Farm Women of Alberta.
- Louise McKinney — first woman to sit in the Legislative Assembly of Alberta, and the first woman elected to a legislature in Canada and the British Empire.

Who were the Famous Five?

The Famous Five, also called the Valiant Five, were: Nellie McClung from Chatsworth, Ontario; Emily Murphy from Cookstown, Ontario; Henrietta Muir Edwards from Montreal; Irene Parlby from London, England; and Louise McKinney from Frankville, Ontario. Each of these women was a pioneer in the cause of the political rights of Canadian women. In 1927, they collectively challenged the Supreme Court of Canada to answer the question, "Does the word *Persons* in section 24 of the British North America Act of 1867 include females?" The Supreme Court's negative response was overturned by the Privy Council in Britain. The Famous Five's successful fight to have women legally recognized as persons threw down gender barriers that had barred women from, among other things, serving as magistrates or being appointed to the Senate of Canada.

Who led the fight for women's rights in Quebec?

The province of Quebec lagged behind the rest of Canada in granting women political rights. Male opposition to female suffrage was supported by one of the greatest powers in Quebec, the Roman Catholic Church. The most outspoken feminist leader in the struggle against almost impossible odds was Marie Thérèse Forget Casgrain. As the head of the League for Women's Rights she saw Quebec women finally get the right to vote in 1940. She became the first female leader of a Canadian political party in 1951 when she was chosen as leader of the Quebec wing of the Co-operative Commonwealth Federation (CCF), the forerunner of the New Democratic Party.

> **Quickies**
> *Did you know ...*
> * that as a teenager Marie Thérèse Forget went on a trip to Europe with her parents? Her father's business in Paris took longer than he had anticipated, and he had to postpone their voyage home. Had the family kept to their original schedule, they would have been aboard the *Titanic*.

What was Mina Hubbard's claim to fame?

Mina Hubbard (*nee* Benson) was the Canadian wife of American journalist and would-be explorer Leonidas Hubbard. In 1903, Leonidas died of starvation when he became lost in the uncharted interior of Labrador. Mina astounded her contemporaries by announcing that she would make the trip through the wilds of Labrador from North

West River to Ungava Bay as a memorial to her beloved husband. No white man, let alone a petite white woman, had been through that country since James MacLean, a Hudson's Bay Company trader, went through there in 1838. In 1905, with the assistance of four experienced woodsmen, Mina Hubbard not only made the incredible journey, but she also won the race to Ungava Bay with a male rival, explorer Dillon Wallace. Mina kept a journal of her adventure and published it as *A Woman's Way Through Unknown Labrador: An Account of the Exploration of the Nascaupee and George Rivers.*

What did Ethel Dickinson of Newfoundland and Eleanor Baubier of Manitoba have in common?

Both young women were teachers who made heroic efforts to help the sick in their communities during the Spanish Flu epidemic of 1918–19, Ethel in St. John's and Eleanor in a small Saskatchewan village. Both women caught the disease and died. The residents of the Saskatchewan village renamed their community Baubier in Eleanor's honour. Today a monument to Ethel Dickinson's memory can be seen in St. John's.

Why was Dr. Jean Dow honoured by the Chinese government?

In 1895, Dr. Jean Dow of Fergus, Ontario, went to China as a medical missionary. In 1897, she opened the first women's hospital in Honan province. Later she opened two more women's hospitals in Changte. In 1920–21, Dr. Dow saved the lives of hundreds of Chinese children and expectant mothers during a widespread famine. For this she was awarded a medal of honour by the Chinese government. In 1926, she saved the life of a Chinese boy who was in the latter stages of kala azar disease, a malady spread by sand flies, by using a new treatment she had developed herself. Dr. Dow died in China in 1927 from an unnamed illness at the age of 56. Though she is buried in China, her name is inscribed on a family monument in a cemetery in Fergus.

Who was the first Canadian to swim the English Channel?

The first Canadian swimmer to accomplish that feat was Winnie Roach-Leuszler of Port Credit, Ontario. On August 16, 1951, 25-year-old mother of three children completed the swim in 13 hours and 25 minutes. She was within 100 yards of shore when a current washed her back 6.5 miles, and she had to swim that last exhausting leg all over again. In 1999, Winnie received the Order of Ontario. She was also inducted into the Canadian Forces Sports Hall of Fame and the Ontario Swimming Hall of Fame.

What made Marilyn Bell of Toronto a Canadian icon?

On September 8/9, 1954, 16-year-old Marilyn Bell became the first person to swim across Lake Ontario. She started at Youngstown, New York, and came ashore 20 hours and 59 minutes later just west of Toronto's CNE grounds at what is now Marilyn Bell Park. The route across the lake was 32 miles as the crow flies, but due to strong winds and primitive navigational equipment, Marilyn actually had to swim twice that distance. Waves

Quickies
Did you know ...
- Winnie Roach-Leuszler was also enthusiastic about baseball, and in 1957 she became Canada's first female baseball umpire?

Quickies
Did you know ...
- that besides Marilyn Bell, two other women began the cross-Lake Ontario swim that day: Winnie Roach-Leuszler, the first Canadian to swim the English Channel; and American champion long-distance swimmer Florence Chadwick? The Canadian National Exhibition had offered Florence Chadwick a $10,000 prize to swim the lake. Marilyn Bell considered this a snub of Canadian swimmers, and took up the challenge with no promise of prize money. Neither Winnie Roach-Leuszler (boat problems) nor Florence Chadwick (stomach pains) was able to complete the Lake Ontario swim.

were up to 15 feet high, and she was often attacked by lamprey eels. When she finally dragged herself ashore, 300,000 cheering people waited to greet her. Over the next two years, Marilyn Bell became the youngest person to swim the English Channel, and also swam the Strait of Juan de Fuca on Canada's west coast. She has been inducted into Canada's Sports Hall of Fame and the Canadian Swimming Hall of Fame, and has been named one of Canada's top athletes of the twentieth century. In 2002, she was awarded the Order of Ontario.

Who was the first woman appointed to the Supreme Court of Canada?

In 1982, Prime Minister Pierre Elliott Trudeau appointed Bertha Wilson to the Supreme Court of Canada. She already had the distinction of being the first woman appointed to the Court of Appeal for Ontario. Bertha Wilson presided over several sensational cases, but perhaps her most controversial ruling came in 1988 in the case of R. vs. Dr. Henry Morgentaler regarding abortion. Wilson ruled that the existing Canadian law prohibiting abortion was unconstitutional in that it interfered with a woman's rights over her own body.

What did Judge Bertha Wilson say in her ruling?

Judge Wilson stated: "The decision whether to terminate a pregnancy is essentially a moral decision, a matter of conscience. I do not think there is or can be any dispute about that. The question is: whose conscience? Is the conscience of the woman to be paramount or the conscience of the state? I believe, for the reasons I gave in discussing the right to liberty, that in a free and democratic society it must be the conscience of the individual."

What great height did Sharon Wood reach?

On May 20, 1986, 29-year-old Sharon Wood of Halifax became the first North American woman to climb to the summit of Mount Everest. She was part of a 12-person team (no porters) called Everest Light, led by Jim Elzinga of Calgary. The expedition ascended the Chinese side of the mountain. By the time the climbers established a camp 2,000 feet below the summit, most of them were exhausted. Sharon Wood made the final ascent with Dwayne Congdon of Canmore, Alberta. The pair remained at the top of the world for only 20 minutes because an 50-mile-an-hour wind was blowing and it was almost sundown.

Who was the first Canadian woman in space?

Roberta Bondar, born in Sault Ste. Marie, Ontario, in 1945, became the first female Canadian astronaut in January 1992 when she flew aboard the space shuttle *Discovery* to perform life science and material science experiments in the Spacelab. She was only the second Canadian in space, and the first neurologist. Dr. Bondar left the Canadian Space Agency in September 1992 to pursue research. She has degrees in zoology and agriculture from the University of Guelph, experimental pathology from the University of Western Ontario, neurobiology from the University of Toronto, and has been admitted as a Fellow of the Royal College of Physicians and Surgeons of Canada as a specialist in neurobiology. Dr. Bondar has received numerous honorary degrees and appointments, and has been inducted into the Canadian Medical Hall of Fame. She has also received the Order of Canada. In addition to all this, Roberta Bondar is a renowned landscape photographer.

What Canadian astronaut is also
an accomplished musician?

Julie Payette, born in Montreal in 1963, has logged over 465 hours in space. She has flown on the space shuttle *Discovery* and participated in the first manual docking of the shuttle to the International Space Station (ISS). She served as a mission specialist, was responsible for ISS systems and operated the Canadarm (Canadian made robotic arm). She was the first Canadian to participate in an ISS assembly mission, and the first Canadian astronaut to board the ISS. Julie Payette has received numerous honours, including distinction for exceptional achievement by a young engineer from the Canadian Council of Professional Engineers, Ordre National du Quebec, and Chevalier de l'Ordre de la Pleiade de la francophonie. She is also a pianist and vocalist who has performed with the Montreal Symphony Orchestra, the Piacere Vocale in Basel, Switzerland, and the Tafelmusik Baroque Orchestra in Toronto.

**prodigies
of science,
invention,
and medicine**

Why is "Granny Ross" a folk hero in Cape Breton?

Marie-Henriette Lejeune was born in Acadia in 1762. She was forced to move numerous times because of wars, and finally settled in Cape Breton's Bras d'Or region as the wife of a former soldier named James Ross. In an area where there were no university-trained doctors, Marie-Henriette became skilled as a midwife and as a practitioner of home-medicine. She knew how to make healing remedies from plants and herbs, and became famous as a "Granny-doctor." When a smallpox epidemic swept across Cape Breton, Granny Ross not only cared for the sick, but she also fought the disease by inoculating healthy people before they could get sick. Inoculation had been known of in England for several years, but the settlers in Cape Breton were very suspicious of it. Granny Ross had no vaccine. She would scratch the patient with a needle that had been dipped in a smallpox blister. Granny Ross continued to work as a healer well into old age. Her story is now a part of Cape Breton lore.

Who invented a system of writing
for Canadian Native languages?

James Evans was a 22-year-old Methodist missionary who came to Canada from England in 1823. He taught at missionary schools and learned the Ojibwa language. In compiling a grammar of the language, he realized that it frequently employs strings of syllables. Adapting the Roman alphabet to a language that has never had a written form can be very awkward, so Evans created a new system of symbols representing the Ojibwa syllables. He began to use it in translations of Scripture and hymns. However, his church superiors frowned upon this and insisted that only the Roman alphabet be used. By 1840, Evans was at Norway House on Lake Winnipeg as a missionary in the territory of the Hudson's Bay Company. He learned Cree, which is related to Ojibwa, and adapted his syllabic alphabet to it. Soon the Cree men, women, and children in the vicinity of Norway House were learning "birch bark talking." Evans wanted a printing press, but the Hudson's Bay Company would not allow it. To the Company's chagrin, he managed to make one himself. Evans criticized the Company for desecrating the Sabbath and for selling alcohol to the Natives. In 1842, when a Cree companion of Evans was killed in a hunting accident, the Company connived to have Evans charged with murder and sent back to England. He died a broken man before the charges could be investigated. Today his syllabic alphabet is used by almost all First Nations.

Why are David Fife and Charles Saunders heroes to Western Canadian wheat growers?

In the early 1840s a Peterborough, Ontario, farmer named David Fife was the object of ridicule from his neighbours because of experiments he had been conducting to create a strain of wheat suited to the cold Canadian climate. By 1843 he had come up with a new strain called Red Fife that ripened more quickly than other strains and so was adaptable to the short Canadian growing season. It also made high-quality flour. Half a century later Charles Saunders crossed Red Fife with an Indian strain called Hard Red Calcutta and created marquis wheat. It was much more resistant to disease than Red Fife, produced more grains to the bushel, and was ready to harvest in just 100 days. Marquis wheat was introduced in 1907. Within 12 years, 90 percent of Canadian wheat fields were growing marquis.

What Canadian doctor was a personal friend of Abraham Lincoln?

Anderson Ruffin Abbott was the first Canadian-born Black man to graduate from medical school and be licensed to practice medicine. During the American Civil War he went south to serve in the Union Army, and became Surgeon-in-Chief at the Camp Baker military hospital. He was one of only eight Black surgeons in the United States treating wounded soldiers. Dr. Abbott became a personal friend of Abraham Lincoln. After Lincoln's assassination, Mary Todd Lincoln gave Dr. Abbott the plaid shawl he had worn on the day of his first inauguration. Dr.

Abbott returned home after the war, and became the first Black coroner in Canada. His later positions included president of the Wilberforce Educational Institute in Ontario, and Medical Superintendent of Provident Hospital in Chicago. Dr. Abbott once wrote, "I am a Canadian, first and last and all the time, but that did not deter me from sympathizing with a nation struggling to wipe out an inequity."

Who was Canada's first female doctor?

In 1867, Emily Jennings Stowe of Norwich, Ontario, graduated from the New York Medical College for Women, which she had attended because no medical school in Canada would accept female students. The prevailing Victorian attitude was that women were "too delicate" to be doctors and that "proper" women did not concern themselves with things like human anatomy. Emily opened a medical office in Toronto, thus becoming the first woman doctor in Canada. However, the province passed a law that required all American-trained doctors in Ontario to attend a term of lectures at an Ontario medical school and pass a set of examinations. Emily Jennings Stowe and another female medical student, Jennie Trout, attended the lectures and passed the examinations, in spite of the most reprehensible efforts of male teachers and students to humiliate and discourage them. Thanks to her lifelong fight to change attitudes, by the time of Emily's death in 1903, there were over 120 women doctors in Canada.

What time is it?

Since arriving in Canada from Scotland as a youth, Sir Sandford Fleming could, by 1878, boast of a long list of accomplishments. He was co-founder of the Royal Canadian Institute, and a renowned engineer, surveyor, writer, and explorer. However, Fleming is best known as the Father of Standard Time. Before Fleming presented his brilliant idea for global time zones in 1878, people in every community set their clocks by the sun, and therefore there was total chaos as far as things like train schedules were concerned. Fleming's proposal was not without opposition. The International Meridian Conference of 1884 rejected the zones he had laid out. Religious groups denounced the whole idea as contrary to God's law, and accused Fleming of being a communist. Nonetheless, by 1883 all railways in North America had adopted the system, and by 1929 all the major countries in the world had accepted Fleming's time zones.

How did a grocer and fish peddler from Port Perry, Ontario, become a guru of "hands-on-healing"?

Daniel David Palmer, born in Port Perry in 1845, sold groceries and fish before opening up his "magnetic healing" studio in Davenport, Iowa, in 1886. His belief, basically, was that good health depended upon the flow of energy through the spinal cord and nervous system. In 1895, he claimed that he had rediscovered the ancient medical arts of such revered men as Hippocrates. To name his technique, Palmer combined the Greek words for "hands" and "practice" and gave the world "chiropractic." Of course, Palmer was roundly condemned by the medical establishment and even spent time in jail for practicing medicine without a licence. Many doctors still have serious doubts about the benefits of chiropractic, but to millions of people Daniel David Palmer was a hero who suffered so that they might have relief from pain.

Why was Doctor Cluny Macpherson of Newfoundland a hero to the Allied troops of the First World War?

After the Germans unleashed the first chlorine poison gas attacks on the Allies in April 1915, the British War Office put together a committee to find some sort of defence against the terrible new weapon. One of the young men on that committee was Dr. Cluny Macpherson, a medical officer with the Newfoundland Regiment. Several of the devices the committee tested were failures. Then Macpherson came up with an "anti-gas respirator." It had a canvas muzzle and goggles that fitted over the wearer's face, and a clip that pinched the nose closed. The wearer breathed through a tube that carried air to the mouth from a canister on the person's back. The canister contained activated charcoal, which filtered out the chlorine gas. It was a simple device, but it worked, and it saved thousands of lives. For his invention Dr. Cluny was awarded the Companion of the Most Distinguished Order of St. Michael and St George, and the Medal of Merit.

Quickies

Did you know ...

- that after the first lethal gas attacks, a story spread through the Canadian trenches that breathing through a handkerchief soaked in one's own urine was protection from the gas? It actually was not, but the idea gave the men a sense of being able to do something should another gas attack come.

How did Dr. Frederick Banting of Ontario astound American businessmen?

Dr. Banting is credited with being the person most responsible for the discovery of insulin in 1921, though he shared the honours with Charles Best and Dr. John James R. Macleod. American pharmaceutical companies offered Banting huge sums of money for the patent on insulin. They wanted to build an insulin clinic in a large American city, put Banting in charge, and make the lifesaving medication available to diabetics who could afford to pay for it. Banting astounded them when he said that insulin was his gift to the human race, and would be available for everybody who needed it; it would not be a commodity for anybody's personal profit. Banting and Macleod received the Nobel Prize for Medicine. Banting shared his half of the honorarium with Best. Banting also received a knighthood.

Quickies
Did you know ...
- that Banting worked with the Royal Canadian Air Force in studying the physiological effects of high-altitude aerial combat on pilots? On February 21, 1941, Banting was on his way to England to conduct tests on a new flying suit, when he was killed in a plane crash off the coast of Newfoundland.

Where did babies first taste Pablum?

In the late 1920s, Toronto's Hospital for Sick Children was renowned for its surgeons, but like most other hospitals it had a high rate of infant mortality. Three physicians in Sick Kids; Dr. Alan Brown, Dr. Theodore Drake, and Dr. Frederick Tisdall, all from Ontario, believed that poor diet was a major factor in the high rate of illness and death among babies. While they were proponents of breast feeding, they knew that mother's milk lacked iron. They also knew that the first solid food most babies were fed was white bread, which lacked many nutrients. They worked together, and with the assistance of laboratory technician Ruth Herbert and chemist Harry Engel, to develop a nutrient-rich food that would be easy for mothers to prepare and

Canada's Nobel Prize Winners
- Frederick Banting and John James R. Macleod — Medicine, 1923
- Lester B. Pearson — Peace, 1957
- Gerhard Herzberg — Chemistry, 1971
- David Hubel — Medicine, 1981
- Henry Taube — Chemistry, 1983
- John Polanyi — Chemistry, 1986
- Sidney Altman — Chemistry, 1989
- Richard Taylor — Physics, 1990
- Rudolph Marcus — Chemistry, 1992
- Michael Smith — Chemistry, 1993
- Bertram Brockhouse — Physics, 1994
- Robert Mundell — Economics, 1999

for babies to digest. The recipe for their pre-cooked cereal included wheat, corn, oats, wheat germ, brewer's yeast, bone meal, alfalfa leaf, iron, and iron salt. They called it "Pablum" from the Greek word for food, *pabulum*. Pablum was fed to babies in Sick Kids Hospital and then became available to the public in 1931. It was a breakthrough in nutritional science because, among other benefits, it contributed to a decrease in the number of cases of rickets, a crippling childhood disease caused by insufficient Vitamin D. For 25 years the Hospital for Sick Children received a royalty on the sales of Pablum.

When did a vaccine to fight tuberculosis first come to Canada?

Dr. Armand Frappier of Salaberry-de-Valleyfield, Quebec, a graduate of the University of Montreal's medical school, lost his mother to tuberculosis while he was still a teenager. In the early twentieth century tuberculosis was one of the worst killer diseases in the western world, and Frappier devoted his life to fighting it. While studying in France he learned that two students of the legendary Louis Pasteur, Albert Calmette and Camille Guerin, claimed to have developed an anti-tuberculosis vaccine they called BCG. Back in Canada, Frappier, amidst much criticism and with the opposition of many naysayers, promoted the study and testing of BCG. He had almost no funding, but he gained the attention of journalists and politicians. In 1938 he founded *L'Institut de microbiologie* in Montreal (it has since been renamed in his honour) and began the production of the vaccine. Frappier organized campaigns to have babies, Native people, schoolchildren, and people in hospitals vaccinated. BCG, along with improved nutrition and hygiene, and the development of antibiotics, has practically wiped out TB as a killer disease. In 1970, Dr. Frappier and his colleagues also discovered that BCG is instrumental in preventing infant leukemia.

Why do visitors from China regard a house in Gravenhurst, Ontario, as a shrine?

The house in question was the birthplace (in 1890) of Dr. Norman Bethune, a doctor who was a controversial figure in Canada but who became a national hero in the People's Republic of China. Bethune studied medicine at the University of Toronto, and was a stretcher bearer in the First World War until he was wounded. He developed tuberculosis, but recovered after undergoing a radical new treatment. He then moved to Montreal where he specialized in surgery and the treatment of TB. Bethune invented several new surgical instruments. He was very socially conscious, and joined the Communist Party in the belief that it would end poverty. His anti-capitalist opinions angered the medical profession and the Canadian government. In the Spanish Civil War he drove an ambulance for the Republican side, and invented a mobile blood transfusion unit to help save the lives of wounded soldiers. In 1938, Bethune went to China where he became a frontline doctor for the Communist army of Mao Tse-tung in the civil war that was raging there. Bethune was tireless in his work of reorganizing a primitive medical system and training new medics. He undoubtedly saved thousands of lives before he died from a septic infection. Today Norman Bethune is highly honoured as a hero in China, and has been recognized in Canada as "a Canadian of national historical significance." His birthplace in Gravenhurst is a historic site.

Quickies

Did you know ...

- that in 1964, a movie about Dr. Norman Bethune was produced in China? The Canadian Broadcasting Corporation produced a TV dramatization called *Bethune,* starring Donald Sutherland, in 1977. In 1993, a major motion picture was released, cooperatively produced by Canada, China, and France, titled *Bethune: The Making of a Hero,* and again starring Donald Sutherland. In 2006, China Central Television produced a 20-part miniseries about Bethune.

**brave
young
canadians**

Who were the only survivors of the wreck of the *Asia*?

On September 14, 1882, the passenger steamer *Asia* sank in a storm on Georgian Bay. Of more than 124 people who had been aboard the ship, only two survived; 17-year-old Christie Ann Morrison and 18-year-old Douglas Tinkis. The two teenagers found themselves adrift in a lifeboat with the bodies of five men who had died from exposure. They had only one oar, which made manoeuvring the boat extremely difficult. They talked to each other all night to keep from slipping into sleep, and possibly death. With the single oar, Douglas managed to get the boat to an island where he and Christie Ann were found by passing Natives who took them to Parry Sound. The wreck of the *Asia* was a major disaster, so there was quite a sensation over the survival of the two young people. Because she was a girl who had survived where grown men had not, Christie Ann in particular was the object of much public attention. A dramatic photograph of her posing with a lifeline in her hands became famous. She grew to hate the photograph and the publicity because they required her to relive over and over again the most frightening experience of her life.

How did a 14-year-old Nova Scotia boy emerge as a hero from a mining disaster?

On February 21, 1891, an explosion ripped through the coal mine at Springhill, Nova Scotia. Danny Robertson, 14, a pony-driver, was thrown into an empty coal car by the force of the blast. When he climbed out, his coat was on fire and his hands and arms were badly burned. He tore off the coat, and then began to stumble through the dark tunnel. He found 12-year-old Willie Terris cringing under the chair he sat on for his job as a trapper — opening and closing the door of a ventilation shaft. Willie had been only slightly burned, but was paralyzed with fear. Another explosion could have rocked the mine at any moment, but Danny took the time to help Willie. His hands were too badly burned for him to carry the boy, so he convinced Willie to climb on his back. Danny carried Willie piggyback until they met a group of rescue workers on their way down into the pit. Danny gave Willie to them, then turned around and was about to go back and look for his older brother, when he was told his brother was safe. When Danny walked out of the mine, he declined the offer of a sleigh ride home. He said he would walk, because he didn't want to worry his mother. Of the 125 workers killed in that disaster, 30 were teenage boys.

What 15-year-old Canadian boy was a hero of the *Lusitania* disaster?

On May 7, 1915, a German submarine torpedoed the passenger liner *Lusitania* 12 miles off the southern coast of Ireland. The great ship sank within a matter of minutes, leaving hundreds of people struggling in the water. One of the 360 Canadians on board was Robert Holt, the teenage son of Sir Herbert Bolt, president of the Royal Bank of Canada. Bob was en route from New York to his school in England. When the ship was hit, Bob grabbed a life jacket and went to the port side. He saw that lifeboats were being capsized as soon as they were launched, so he rushed to the starboard rail. People there were climbing down the side of the sinking ship and grabbing onto anything that would keep them afloat. Bob was about to go over the side when he saw a woman who did not have a life jacket. In a true act of gallantry, Bob Holt took his life jacket off and gave it to the woman. Then he went over the side. Bob was a strong swimmer, and he swam from one clutch of survivors to another until he found an upside-down lifeboat with 30 people on it. He asked if there was room for one more, and a man helped him climb on. They were among the lucky ones who were rescued. The *Lusitania* disaster cost 1,189 lives. German newspapers celebrated the sinking of the *Lusitania*. Canadian newspapers told of the selfless boy who gave away his life jacket.

What act of courage did Agnes Foran perform in the aftermath of the Halifax Explosion?

On the morning of December 6, 1917, a ship loaded with munitions exploded in Halifax Harbour. The blast was the biggest man-made, non-nuclear explosion in history, and much of the city of Halifax was levelled. Almost 2,000 were killed. In their home on Merkel Street, 12-year-old Agnes Foran and her mother were looking out the window when suddenly "the sky opened." The windows blew in and Agnes and her mother were thrown to the floor. Agnes got up and found that her mother had been blinded by flying glass. She took her mother out to the street, and then went back into the house to rescue her baby brother. Agnes, who was covered in blood herself, then went up and down the ruined streets in search of help. Finding none, she returned to her mother and brother. Finally, Agnes's father, who had been at work, returned. He took his family to the hospital. There, doctors found that a piece of glass half the size of an adult's hand had been driven into Agnes's stomach, with only a tiny point visible above the skin. Surgery was necessary to remove the glass, and it took 29 stitches to close the wound. Agnes fully recovered.

Who was the "Hurricane Baby"?

On the night of October 16, 1954, Hurricane Hazel swept down upon Toronto, bringing with it millions of tons of precipitation and causing massive flooding. One of the many dramas played out that terrifying night took place on

Four Other Young Heroes of the Halifax Explosion

Eight-year-old Norman Roberts carried his baby sister out of their shattered, burning apartment building, then went back in and dragged out his unconscious mother. Cecelia McGrath, 11, led eight other girls out of the ruins of St. Joseph's Catholic School. Roland Theakson, 14, calmly told 35 small boys of the Bloomfield School, which had lost its roof and windows, to exit the building according to the fire drill they had practiced, and got all of them safely outside. Nine-year-old Pearl Hartlen found her unconscious mother under the debris of their wrecked home. She started to pull her mother free, but Mrs. Hartlen's skirt was caught on something. Pearl had nothing to cut with, so she bit and tore at the fabric until she could pull her mother out and drag her to safety.

Island Road. Etobicoke Creek had become a raging torrent, overflowing its banks and forcing local residents to the roofs of their houses. Perched on the roof of one house was the Thorpe family: Clifford, Patricia, two-year-old Billy, four-month-old Nancy, and Patricia's mother. Chief Albert Houston of the Long Branch Fire Department managed to reach the house in a small boat and take baby Nancy to another, more solid house, where people were gathered on the roof. He gave the child to 16-year-old Sylvia Jones. When Houston went back for the rest of the Thorpe family, they had all been swept away by the flood. Sylvia clung to little Nancy all night long, trying to keep the baby warm with her own shivering body. In the morning, the people were taken off the roof in the shovel of a bulldozer. Nancy was taken to St. Joseph's Hospital, where nobody knew who she was. She was simply the "Hurricane Baby" until her paternal grandparents recognized her picture in the paper and claimed her.

How did Jocelyn McDonald become one of the youngest recipients of Canada's Star of Courage?

On the afternoon of April 25, 1992, seven-year-old Jocelyn McDonald and a five-year-old girlfriend were confronted by an adult male who told them to take off their underpants. When they did not, the man grabbed the five-year-old and carried her off. Jocelyn knew who the man was and where he lived. She followed them to his house. She sneaked inside, and while the man was occupied in the bathroom, she searched the house until she found her small friend. The little girl was in a bedroom, still dressed but too frightened to move. Jocelyn took the girl by the hand and both children fled the house. At first they were reluctant to tell anyone what had happened, but the story came out when the same man was accused of assaulting another child. For her courage, Jocelyn McDonald received the Star of Courage from Governor General Ray Hnatyshyn. Tragically, in the year 2000, Jocelyn was murdered.

Why is Craig Kielburger (born 1982 in Thornhill, Ontario) in this chapter?

Craig Kielburger is no longer a kid, but he is a children's rights advocate, and as co-founder with his brother Marc of Free the Children and Leaders Today, he enables children to become heroes by voluntarily helping other children around the world. Under his leadership, Free the Children has built more than 500 elementary schools. Kielburger is a renowned author and an influential speaker who has travelled to more than 70 countries to speak in defence of children's rights. His work has drawn the attention of the United Nations, Oprah Winfrey, the Dalai Lama, Bill Clinton, Nelson Mandela, Archbishop Desmond Tutu, and Queen Noor of Jordan.

Craig Kielburger's Awards

- Order of Canada
- Ontario Medal for Good Citizenship
- Nelson Mandela Human Rights Award
- 2006 World Children's Prize
- Community of Christ International Peace Award
- State of the World Forum Award
- Reebok Human Rights Award
- Medal of Meritorious Service
- Roosevelt Freedom Award
- 2005 Kiwanis World Service Medal

in the
line of duty

Who was the first known Canadian firefighter to be killed in the line of duty?

Between midnight and one o'clock on November 22, 1848, the bells of St. James Church on King Street in Toronto alerted the city's volunteer fire department of a blaze right across the road. The fire started in a shoe store and spread to a saddle store, a hat shop, and a dry goods store. The volunteers put two pumpers into action, and by 3:00 a.m. they had the fire under control. However, a falling stone windowsill struck fireman William Thornton on the head, fracturing his skull. He was taken to the fire hall where a doctor cleaned the wound and bled him. He was then taken to his home, where he died two days later.

Who was the hero of the Parliament Building fire?

On the evening of February 3, 1916, fire broke out in the Reading Room of the House of Commons in the Parliament Building in Ottawa. Seven people died in that conflagration, and national treasures and priceless works of art were destroyed. The fire reduced North America's finest example of gothic architecture to a smoking shell. Prime Minister Sir Robert Borden was among the survivors. The death toll would certainly have been higher had it not been for the heroics of Chief Engineer Thomas Wensley. In spite of the flames, smoke, and the risk to his own life, he rushed down to a boiler room and shut off a steam system that could have caused a devastating explosion.

> **Quickies**
> *Did you know ...*
> - that over 900 Canadian firefighters have been killed in the line of duty or have died from health problems directly related to firefighting?

What incident caused the greatest single loss of Canadian firefighters' lives?

On December 6, 1917, the Halifax Fire Department responded when informed that a ship was on fire in the harbour. This was the French munitions ship *Mont Blanc,* which was loaded with explosives. Several firemen raced to the harbour in Halifax's only motorized fire engine, a brand new vehicle they had named *Patricia.* Chief Edward Condon and Deputy Chief William Brunt followed in a car. As they neared the harbour, the *Mont Blanc* blew up. Among the nearly 2,000 fatalities caused by the Halifax Explosion were nine firefighters. Chief Condon, Assistant Chief Brunt, Captain William Broderick, Captain George

Twenty-one Other Dates and Locations at Which Three or More Firefighters Were Killed in the Line of Duty		
Date	Place	Number Killed
April 29, 1877	Montreal	5
April 25, 1878	Cobourg, Ontario	3
October 16, 1896	Montreal	3
July 10, 1902	Toronto	5
June 22, 1913	Montreal	4
May 10, 1918	Vancouver	5
December 23, 1926	Winnipeg	4
June 17, 1932	Montreal	4
July 23, 1934	Toronto	3
June 25, 1937	Montreal	3
June 2, 1940	Edmundston, New Brunswick	6
May 17, 1947	Toronto	3
May 19, 1951	Peterborough, Ontario	3
October 16, 1954	Toronto	5
March 2, 1960	Montreal	5
March 12, 1961	Quebec City	3
April 6, 1963	Montreal	3
December 4, 1978	Etobicoke, Ontario	3
March 19, 1981	Iroquois, ON	5
May 15, 1981	Montreal	3
June 27, 1993	Warwick, Quebec	4

Maltis, and firemen John Spruin, Walter Hennessey, Frank Kileen, and John Duggan were all killed instantly. Fireman Frank Leahy was badly injured and died six days later.

How did Hurricane Hazel take the lives of five Toronto firemen?

When Hurricane Hazel struck Toronto on the night of October 16, 1954, the 70-mile-per-hour winds that came shrieking across Lake Ontario certainly were frightful, but the greatest danger was caused by the 300 million tons of rain that fell on ground already saturated from three weeks of steady precipitation. It wasn't the wind that made Hurricane Hazel a killer, it was the flooding. Rescue workers spent long, dangerous hours pulling people out of raging rivers and creeks, and plucking them from the roofs of houses. In one tragic incident, the rescuers became the victims. Six members of the Kingsway-Lambton Volunteer Fire Department roared off in their fire engine in response to a call about some people trapped on a rooftop. The roads of Toronto had been turned into rivers. The six-ton fire engine was caught in a wash so powerful, it rolled over. Five of the men: Clarence Collins, Frank Mercer, Roy Oliver, David Palmeter, and Angus Small were drowned. A plaque commemorates their sacrifice.

Quickies
Did you know ...
• Hurricane Hazel killed 83 Torontonians? Of those, 38 were from Raymore Drive, a street that ran parallel to the Humber River and was virtually washed off the map. It would be remembered as "The street that never was" and "Calamity Crescent."

Who was the hero of a daring, mid-Atlantic helicopter rescue?

In January 1980, three men were trapped aboard the crippled freighter *Bill Crosbie* in the midst of a savage Atlantic storm, hundreds of miles off the coast of Newfoundland. The ship was in danger of sinking, and raging seas made it impossible for other vessels to get near enough to take the men off. Rescue came in the form of a big Labrador long-distance helicopter dispatched from the Search and Rescue (SAR) base at Gander, Newfoundland. Because the ship kept rising and falling on mountainous swells, and gale-force winds blew the helicopter all over the sky, the rescue was exceedingly difficult. Search and Rescue technician Dave Maloley dangled by a cable beneath the helicopter while Captain Rudy Preus fought to hold the aircraft steady. Maloley slammed into the ship's funnel and received powerful electric shocks when he became entangled with the ship's antenna. In spite of horrific conditions, the SAR team got the men off the ship and landed them safely in St. John's. Dave Maloley was awarded the Star of Courage.

How did a Cape Breton fire chief earn the Star of Courage?

On December 16, 1984, two young boys attempted to cross the frozen surface of Big Pond between the communities of Sydney Mines and Florence, Nova Scotia. They went through the ice about 200 metres from shore. The Sydney Mines Fire Department was alerted and Chief John Nugent responded, along with fireman Donald MacPherson. Neither had any training in water rescue. One boy had already gone under. Nugent crawled out onto the dangerously thin ice to try to get to the other boy. Just as Nugent got hold of the unconscious boy, he went through the ice, too. Macpherson also broke through when he tried to go to Chief Nugent's assistance. In spite of the numbingly cold water, Nugent held onto the boy until all three were pulled into a small rescue boat. The boy was taken to a Halifax hospital where he recovered. Chief John Nugent was awarded the Star of Courage by Governor General Jeanne Sauvé on March 21, 1986. The new Sydney Mines Fire Hall has been named in his honour.

How did a blocked sewer drain lead to an explosion in a Canadian castle?

The Villeneuve Castle was a local landmark in Picton, Ontario. It was built between 1805 and 1811, and then enlarged in 1860. It was a compact castle with four turrets, 25 rooms, a grand ballroom, and an elegant staircase. In 1986 the Villeneuve had a high-class restaurant that was considered the best place to dine for miles around. During the days leading up to January 11 of that year, the weather had been quite cold, and a sewer drain in the basement had frozen. That evening, workmen were using an industrial propane heater to try to thaw the drain. Propane gas leaked into the basement and then exploded. The blast ripped upwards through the castle with the power of 200 pounds of TNT. The hardwood floors from ground level to the third storey were blown to kindling, as were the roof timbers. Turrets fell inward, and huge timbers crashed downwards. Large sections of the stone walls fell in, and were supported only by unstable debris. Fires burned everywhere, and there was still the smell of gas in the air. Police and members of the Picton Volunteer Fire Department were quickly on the scene. Without hesitation, Deputy Chief Reg Havery and firemen Paul Bartlett and Bill Harvey crawled into the debris to rescue several injured people who had been trapped. This was extremely dangerous because the walls could have fallen on them at any moment, or the gas floating around them could have ignited. At great risk to their own lives, the firemen got the injured people out. One person was killed in the Villeneuve Castle explosion, and 14 were seriously injured. Havery, Bartlett, and Harvey were all awarded the Star of Courage.

civilian heroes

How did Sid Choquette become a hero in Frank, Alberta?

In the early morning of April 29, 1903, a huge rockfall from Turtle Mountain struck the town of Frank. Engineer Ben Murgatroyd saw the avalanche of rocks coming toward him in time to get his train out of the way, but now the tracks were buried under 100 feet of rock. A passenger train from Lethbridge was due any minute, and the engineer would not see the danger until it was too late. Two brakemen, Sid Choquette and Bill Lowes, climbed onto the mountain of rocks and began to run toward the other side so they could warn the oncoming train. It was an extremely dangerous run. The rocks were sharp, unstable underfoot, and still hot from friction. The men had to dodge boulders that still came hurtling down the mountain, and they were choking from the lime dust that filled the air. Lowes finally dropped from exhaustion, unable to go on, but Choquette kept going. When he staggered down the other side of the mound of rubble, by good luck he was right at the spot where the rails emerged from the debris. He ran up the line waving a lantern. The engineer of the approaching train saw the signal light in the darkness and brought the train to a stop. Another few minutes, and a disastrous train wreck would have added to the tragic human toll of the Frank Slide.

What Montreal principal sacrificed her life for the children in her school?

On the afternoon of February 26, 1907, fire broke out in the Hochelaga Protestant School in Montreal. The cause was apparently an overheated furnace in the basement. As soon as they were aware of the smoke, the teachers on the ground floor managed to get their pupils out in good order. Sarah Maxwell, the school's 31-year-old principal, was on the ground floor and might easily have

Quickies

Did you know ...

- that a story circulated that the grateful Canadian Pacific Railway rewarded Sid Choquette with a gold watch? Actually, the CPR gave Choquette $25 and a letter of commendation.

escaped. Instead she went upstairs where the kindergarten class was to help evacuate the third floor. Some of the small children got out, but the fire spread through the building so rapidly that the narrow stairway became impassable. Now Sarah Maxwell and the children were trapped on the top floor, and there was no fire escape. Firemen arrived and put ladders up to the kindergarten classroom window. Sarah started passing children out. As flames and smoke filled the room behind her, it seemed as though Sarah was about to finally climb out herself. Then she told the fireman at the top of the ladder, "There must still be children inside." She went back in, though the fireman called to her to come back. He tried to go in after her, but was driven back by heat and smoke. The firemen took about 45 minutes to get the blaze under control. When they went inside, they found the bodies of Sarah Maxwell and 17 children. Sarah had evidently been trying to carry a child to the window when she was overcome by smoke. When the school was rebuilt, it was named in her honour. Another teacher, identified only as Miss Campbell, was awarded a gold medal for the coolness and bravery she displayed in getting her students out of the school.

When did a future movie star become an unsung hero following a Canadian disaster?

On June 30, 1912, a tornado ripped through Regina, Saskatchewan. Within five minutes the whirlwind had torn a swath of destruction three blocks wide and 12 blocks long. At least 28 people were dead and the damage was in the millions of dollars. More than 3,000 people were suddenly homeless. At the time the tornado struck, a young English actor named William Henry Pratt was enjoying a day off by paddling a canoe in Wascana Lake. His troupe had made a stop in Regina and he was lodged in a boarding house. Pratt was not hurt in the tornado, but his boarding house was demolished. Regina was not his town, but the actor rolled up his sleeves and joined the local people in the colossal task of cleaning up the debris. Then he and his fellow thespians put on a benefit performance to raise money for tornado victims. This little-known hero of the disastrous Regina tornado would one day terrify audiences as the Frankenstein monster, which he played under his stage name, Boris Karloff.

How did "Doc" MacLean thwart a bank robbery in New Hazelton, British Columbia?

Donald "Doc" MacLean was a veterinarian and a preacher. He was also a crack shot with a rifle and a man with nerves of steel. On April 8, 1914, a gang of Russian bandits entered New Hazelton to rob the bank. Several months earlier the same gang had robbed the New Hazelton bank and had killed a clerk. This time they had Doc MacLean to contend with. He grabbed his rifle and shot it out with the outlaws. By the time the gun smoke cleared, two of the bandits were dead and four were wounded. Only the bandit leader managed to escape.

Who were the heroes of the *Empress of Ireland* disaster?

Early in the morning of May 29, 1914, the ocean liner *Empress of Ireland* collided with the Norwegian freighter *Storstad* in the St. Lawrence River. The liner's hull was ripped open and she began to sink quickly in the frigid water. It was the worst marine disaster in Canadian history, costing the lives of 1,012 people. There were, however, acts of heroism. Sir Henry Seton-Karr, a famous big game hunter, forcibly put his life jacket on a man who didn't have one. Sir Henry drowned. Dr. Jonas Grant, the ship's doctor, lost his clothes when he squeezed out through a porthole, and was naked when he was pulled into a lifeboat. He asked for a pair of pants and then went straight to work treating injured and shock-stricken survivors. Robert Crellin of British Columbia was in the water when he took eight-year-old Florence Barbour on his back. The little girl lost both her parents in the shipwreck, so Crellin and his wife adopted her. There had been 138 children aboard the ship. Florence was one of only four who survived.

How did a projectionist and an usher become heroes during Canada's worst movie theatre fire?

On the afternoon of January 9, 1927, fire broke out on the balcony of Montreal's Laurier Palace movie theatre. The audience was mostly unchaperoned children. At the cry of "Fire!" the ground floor was quickly evacuated. But up on the balcony all was chaos. Terrified children rushed for the two narrow stairways. At the west stairway a young usher named Paul Champagne, who had not immediately fled his post as the other ushers had done, took charge. Champagne made the children exit down the stairs and out to the street in an orderly manner. Having saved the lives of one group of children, Champagne tried to go back for the others, but was blocked by thick smoke. Meanwhile, projectionist Emile Massicote looked out of his small projection room and saw the crush of children trying to push their way through the east stairway door. The projection room had a window that opened onto the theatre's marquee. Massicote shouted that he had a way out, but the shrieking, hysterical children didn't hear him. Massicote grabbed two screaming, kicking children, dragged them to the window, and put them out on the marquee. Then he went back for two more. Massicote rescued 30 children before the heavy smoke forced him to climb out onto the marquee himself. The Laurier Palace theatre fire killed 78 children; a tragedy that would have been even worse but for the heroics of an usher and a projectionist.

Who was the *Noronic*'s "Eddy"?

When fire broke out aboard the Great Lakes passenger liner *Noronic* in Toronto Harbour early on the morning of September 17, 1949, only a skeleton crew was aboard and most of the passengers were asleep in their staterooms. The fire spread through the ship rapidly, and several of the crew on night duty hurried ashore without alerting the passengers. However, a bellboy identified only as Eddy did not shirk his duty. As soon as he was aware of the fire he ran to a cabin on A-deck where other bellboys were sleeping and awakened them. Eddy and two of the boys

On January 25, 1978, in Summerside, Prince Edward Island, 25-year-old Freddy Gaudet murdered storekeeper Harold Arsenault with a shotgun. Gaudet had been indulging in alcohol and marijuana. He ran into Smallman's clothing store where he took several women hostage. One young woman started to run, and Gaudet raised the shotgun as though to shoot her. Debbie McInnis, a 21-year-old employee, seized the gun. There was a desperate struggle as Gaudet fought to get control of the weapon and McInnis refused to let go. Then the gun went off, blowing a hole in the floor. Gaudet fled, leaving McInnis holding the shotgun. Gaudet ran into Holman's department store where he armed himself with another shotgun and took yet another group of women hostage. Police surrounded the place, but could not move in because Gaudet was holding the gun at the head of a young woman named Debbie MacLean. Then one officer thought he saw a trigger-guard on Gaudet's shotgun. The police decided to rush the killer. When they made their move, Gaudet aimed the gun at Officer Harold Durant. But just as he did so, Debbie MacLean grabbed the shotgun by the barrel and pushed it away. That gave the officers the split second they needed to subdue Gaudet. As it turned out, the trigger-guard on the shotgun was defective, and Gaudet could have fired the gun. Debbie McInnis and Debbie MacLean were both awarded the American Carnegie Medal for bravery and the Star of Courage.

How did John King of Winnipeg become a hero?

On June 2, 1987, a man and his four-year-old son Rene were among several people fishing in the Red River from Winnipeg's North Main-Perimeter boat launch. The river bottom there drops away steeply just a few feet from shore. There had not been many warm days that spring, so the water was still quite cold. It began to rain slightly, but most of the people continued to fish. However, the father was concerned that the rain might come down harder at any moment. He and the boy went to the parking lot and got into their station wagon. The father backed the car down the concrete boat ramp and put it in park. He left Rene sitting on the front seat while he opened the tailgate, sat on it, and resumed fishing. Little Rene decided to pretend he was driving, and he put the car into neutral. Suddenly it was rolling backwards into the river. The startled father, who could not swim, scrambled onto the roof. Realizing the danger, he hung over the side and tried to open the door, but the water pressure was too great. He shouted to Rene to roll the window down, but the child ignored him. The car was sinking lower into the river. In desperation the father shouted for help. Standing on the shore fishing was 39-year-old John King. When King saw what was happening he did not hesitate even to take off his heavy work boots. He dove right in and swam for the car. While some men hauled the father ashore with a rope, King swam into the open back of the station wagon and got Rene out. But his own sodden clothing and boots were a hindrance, and the icy water was probably sapping his strength quickly. Another man, Robert Pourier, kicked off his shoes and dove into the river. When Pourier got close enough, King handed Rene to him. Everyone was watching Pourier fight the current to get the boy ashore. No one saw John King go under. RCMP officers recovered his body later that day. King was posthumously awarded the Star of Courage.

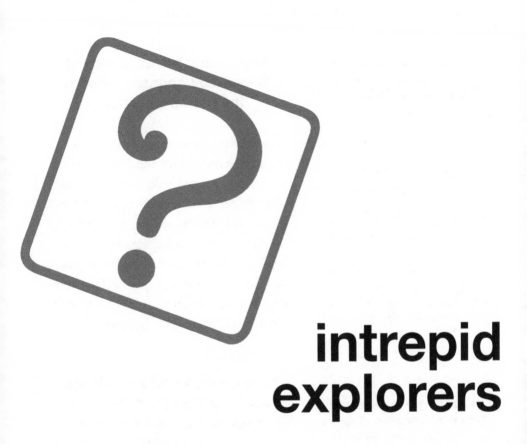

intrepid explorers

Seven Explorers of Canada Who Disappeared While on Expeditions of Discovery

- John Cabot, 1498, off Canada's east coast
- Gaspar Corte-Real, 1501, off Canada's east coast
- Miguel Corte-Real (Gaspar's brother), 1502, off Canada's east coast
- John Knight, 1606, Labrador
- Henry Hudson, 1611, James Bay
- James Knight, 1719, Canadian Arctic
- Sir John Franklin, 1847. Canadian Arctic

Why should the explorers of Canada be counted among the nation's heroes?

Whatever their motivations, the explorers were courageous individuals who dared to venture into the unknown. Bit by bit, often under conditions that would have made those with fainter hearts turn back, they filled in the blank spaces on the maps. Few of them gained the wealth or glory they hungered for, and some of them died with their boots on while trying to find out what lay beyond the horizon.

Twelve Canadian Geographical Features Named After Explorers

- Frobisher Bay — Martin Frobisher
- Baffin Island — William Baffin
- Davis Strait — John Davis
- Lake Champlain — Samuel de Champlain
- Mackenzie River — Alexander Mackenzie
- Vancouver Island — George Vancouver
- Thompson River — David Thompson
- Fraser River — Simon Fraser
- Hudson Bay — Henry Hudson
- Hudson Strait — Henry Hudson
- Cabot Strait — John Cabot
- Mont Jacques Cartier — Jacques Cartier

How do we know the Vikings were the first Europeans to explore the east coast of Canada?

Norse sagas tell us that about the year 1000, Viking leaders like Leif Ericsson and Thorfinn Karlsefini sailed from Iceland and Greenland and landed at places they called Helluland, Markland, and Vinland. Historians disagree on the exact locations for these place names, but suggest Helluland could have been Baffin Island or Labrador, Markland could have been Newfoundland, and Vinland could have been Nova Scotia. Archeological finds at L'Anse aux Meadows in Newfoundland prove beyond a doubt that the Vikings had a settlement there.

Who Was John Cabot?

He was actually Giovanni Caboto, a Genoese mariner who in 1496 convinced King Henry VII of England that he could do for the English what another Italian, Christopher Columbus, had failed to do for the Spanish; reach China by sailing west. On his historic voyage in 1497, Cabot made a landfall in North America. The site is still disputed. It could have been the coast of Maine, mainland Nova Scotia, Cape Breton Island, Newfoundland, or Labrador. Cabot called his discovery the "new-found-land." A year later, Cabot set out on another voyage and vanished from history.

Quickies
Did you know ...
- that after the earliest Spanish and Portuguese expeditions to the "New World," the pope divided the entire Western Hemisphere, from the North Pole to the South Pole, between Spain and Portugal? When the monarchs of those countries learned of the Cabot voyage, they sent strong warnings to King Henry to keep out of their territory. Henry ignored the threats. It is possible that Cabot's 1498 expedition, which mysteriously vanished, might have run into an expedition led by Alonso de Ojeda, an utterly ruthless adventurer sent out by King Ferdinand of Spain to look for gold and silver, and kill anyone he caught trespassing in "Spanish" waters.

Why were European monarchs so anxious to find a western sea route to China?

Europeans wanted the silks, spices, and other items that could be had only in trade with the Far East. Italian city states like Venice and Florence had that trade locked up tight, and charged exorbitant prices for the merchandise. The monarchs and merchants in other European countries thought that if they could find a new sea route to China, they could bypass the Italian middlemen and enrich themselves. The person who found that sea route would be showered with honours and riches.

What was the reaction of the European explorers when they "discovered" the New World?

More than anything they wanted to find a way around it. Their primary goal was still to find a commercially viable sea route to China, and it would remain so for 400 years.

What were Jacques Cartier's accomplishments?

Jacques Cartier's greatest accomplishment was the discovery of the St. Lawrence River in 1535. He explored it as far as the site of Montreal in hope that it would lead to the Pacific Ocean. Cartier also made the first territorial claims that were the beginning of a French empire in North America. He discovered Prince Edward Island, proved that Newfoundland is an island (previous explorers had thought it was part of the mainland), and learned of a Native cure for scurvy made from the leaves and bark of white cedar — a cure that was subsequently lost.

Quickies

Did you know ...

- that it was Cartier who gave Canada its name? He heard an Iroquois call his community *kanata,* the Iroquoian word for village. Cartier thought it was the name of the entire country.

Why is Samuel de Champlain called "The Father of New France" and "The Father of Canada"?

Samuel de Champlain battled against the odds to establish a permanent French colony in the New World even though previous attempts had failed. In 1608, he founded Quebec City. Without that colony there would have been no Canada as we know it. Champlain was the first explorer to probe the wilderness of Quebec and Ontario, and he laid the foundations for the all-important fur trade. Though he was forced to surrender a besieged and starving Quebec to English privateers in 1629, he returned in 1633 to rebuild the French colony. It was a thriving community by the time Champlain died in 1635.

Quickies

Did you know ...

- Cartier found what he thought were diamonds and took a bushel of them back to France? They turned out to be worthless quartz. This resulted in a new catch-phrase in France: *faux comme les diamants du Canada* — "as false as Canadian diamonds."

How did Champlain make the Iroquois the arch-enemies of New France?

In 1609, Champlain and two or three other Frenchmen used their firearms to help their Huron, Algonquin, and Montagnais friends defeat their Iroquois enemies. In 1615, Champlain and a dozen or so French soldiers joined a Huron invasion of the Iroquois homeland on the south shore of Lake Ontario. Their attack on an Iroquois town failed, and the invaders withdrew. Champlain was wounded in the fighting and had to be carried in a basket. The Iroquois never forgave the French.

> **Quickies**
> *Did you know ...*
> • that in 1606 Champlain tried to establish a colony at Port Royal (now Annapolis Royal), Nova Scotia? To fight the boredom of the long winter, he instituted the Order of Good Cheer, which required the colonists to take turns entertaining each other with feasts and performances. This was Canada's first social club.

Who was "the Columbus of the Great Lakes"?

Étienne Brûlé was a protégé of Samuel de Champlain, and the first European who could actually be called a frontiersman. Champlain sent young Brûlé to live among the Natives to learn their languages and their customs. Brûlé readily took to life in the wilderness. He travelled widely with the Natives, and there is evidence that he was the first European to see all of the Great Lakes except Lake Michigan. This has led some historians to call him "the Columbus of the Great Lakes."

Why are there uncertainties about Brûlé's discoveries?

Brûlé kept no known records of his own, but seems to have passed all of his information on to Champlain. In 1629, for reasons still disputed, Brûlé assisted the English in their capture of Quebec, and Champlain damned him as a traitor. Rather than give his former companion credit, Champlain may have claimed some of Brûlé's discoveries for himself. Also, the Jesuit priests who were important chroniclers of the early days of New France hated Brûlé because they considered him immoral and unchristian. In their journals Brûlé is generally referred to as a "wretch."

What was the most infamous mutiny in Canadian history?

The most infamous act of mutiny in Canadian history was that of the crew of the *Discovery* against Captain Henry Hudson in 1611. It made a tragic hero out of Hudson, and added an intriguing mystery to Canada's Arctic lore.

Why did Henry Hudson's crew mutiny?

When Henry Hudson sailed his ship *Discovery* through the Hudson Strait (known then as the Furious Overfall) and into Hudson Bay in 1610, he thought he had reached the Pacific Ocean. The ship was trapped at the bottom of James Bay by ice, and the crew spent a hellish winter. In spring, when the ice finally went out of the bay, the starving survivors wanted to go back to England. Hudson told the men they were going to continue searching for the route to China. A group of conspirators seized control of the ship. They put Hudson, his teenaged son, a few sick men, and any crewmen who were loyal to the captain into a boat and set it adrift. The fate of Hudson and his fellow castaways remains a mystery.

What was Henry Kelsey's great accomplishment?

In the early1690s, Kelsey became the first European to travel inland from Hudson Bay to the Canadian prairies. This was an important step in expanding the fur trade and opening up the interior of the continent. Kelsey also proved that a European could survive in the wilderness by adapting to Native ways.

What protégé of Captain James Cook has a major Canadian city named after him?

James Cook is considered one of the greatest explorers and navigators of all time, and he was mentor to young George Vancouver. Vancouver sailed with Cook, witnessed his death at the hands of Hawaiian natives, and for the rest of his life held Cook as his idol.

How did Vancouver make his own mark in history?

The Tragic Fates of 10 Explorers of Canada

- Sir Humphrey Gilbert — drowned when his ship the *Squirrel* went down with all hands on a return voyage from Newfoundland, 1583.
- Martin Frobisher — died in Plymouth, England, of infection after being shot in the thigh during a fight with the French, 1594.
- Étienne Brûlé — murdered by Natives, possibly eaten, near Penetanguishene, Ontario, 1633.
- Robert de La Salle — murdered by mutineers in Texas, 1687.
- Pierre Radisson — died in extreme poverty in London, England, 1710.
- James Cook — killed in confrontation with Natives, Hawaiian Islands, 1779.
- Dionisio Alcala Galiano — decapitated by a cannonball at the Battle of Trafalgar, 1805.
- Joseph René Bellot — went through the ice in Wellington Channel, Canadian Arctic, 1853.
- David Thompson — died in extreme poverty in Longueuil, Lower Canada (Quebec), 1857.
- Charles Francis Hall — died from illness, possibly poisoned, Greenland, 1871.

In the early 1790s, Captain Vancouver charted much of the west coast of North America. He also proved that the island named after him is in fact an island. Previously Europeans had thought Vancouver Island was an extension of the mainland. Historians have said that of all the marine surveyors who trained under the great Captain Cook, only George Vancouver was in the same class as the master.

Who was known as "The Man Who Mapped the West"?

David Thompson of London, England, came to Canada while just a boy as an apprentice with the Hudson's Bay Company. A fellow employee taught him the basics of surveying, and this became the love of Thompson's life. In 1797 he went over to the rival North West Company which expressed more interest in exploration than the Hudson's Bay Company had. Over the next 15 years, usually under extremely primitive conditions, Thompson surveyed and mapped more territory than any individual explorer had done before him. It was a feat that would not be matched by anyone who came after. There were several occasions when Thompson was fortunate to emerge from the wilderness alive. At the age of 43, Thompson went to Montreal to work on his masterpiece, his "Map of the North-West Territory of the Province of Canada." Thompson's Great Map, as it came to be called, measures 10 feet by 6.5 feet. It shows, in detail, the region between Hudson Bay and the Pacific Ocean, from the Great Lakes and the Columbia River in the south to Lake Athabasca in the north. Thompson had travelled more than 50 thousand miles across that land in order to fill in the empty spaces. By the time of his death in 1857, Thompson was all but forgotten. Today he is recognized as one of the greatest mapmakers who ever lived.

What important scientific discovery was made by Arctic explorer James Clark Ross?

In 1828, British explorer James Clark Ross and his uncle John Ross, both veterans of the Arctic, sailed their ship *Victory* to the Boothia Peninsula, the northernmost extension of mainland Canada. Their ship became trapped in the ice and the two Rosses and their men were stranded for many months. While they awaited a thaw that they hoped would release the ship, James Ross made several journeys by sled. On one of these expeditions he reached a spot where he noticed the needle of a device called a dip circle (a type of compass) was pointing straight down. He realized he was standing above the North Magnetic Pole, the location of which had previously been unknown.

Quickies
Did you know ...
- that from 1816 to 1826 Thompson was "Astronomer and Surveyor" for the British Boundary Commission? He helped to establish the Ontario section of the United States-Canada border.

Why was James Ross's discovery important?

Europeans had known for centuries that a compass needle points only in the general direction of the geographic North Pole, which is the actual true north. What the compass needle points directly at is the geomagnetic North Pole, which is not the same thing. Arctic explorers who had gone before James Ross had noted that in the Arctic their compasses behaved strangely, so they knew the North Magnetic Pole was somewhere in the area. The British believed Ross's discovery important enough that they marked the North Magnetic Pole on their maps. Later it was learned that the North Magnetic pole moves from one location to another. Scientists still do not know why.

Quickies
Did you know ...
- the *Victory* never did get free of the ice, and had to be abandoned? In the summer of 1831 John and James Ross and their crew were rescued by a whaling ship.

When did the first ship successfully navigate the Northwest Passage?

In 1905, Norwegian explorer Roald Amundsen sailed his ship *Gjoa* from east to west through the Northwest Passage. In 1942, the RCMP vessel *St. Roche* became the first ship to successfully navigate the Northwest Passage from west to east.

Who was the first Canadian astronaut?

Marc Garneau, born in Quebec City in 1949, was the first Canadian in space. He had the rank of Commander in the Canadian Navy when in 1984 he was one of six applicants chosen from over 4,000 for the Canadian Astronaut Program. After his initial flight aboard the space shuttle *Challenger* as a payload specialist in 1984, Garneau flew further missions in 1996 and 2000, making him the first Canadian to go into space three times. Captain Garneau logged almost 678 hours in space before he retired as an astronaut. He has been made a Companion of the Order of Canada, and a Toronto high school has been named in his honour. A squadron of the Royal Canadian Air Cadets is also named after Marc Garneau. In the 2008 federal election, Garneau ran as the Liberal candidate for the riding of Westmount-Ville-Marie, and won by more than 9,000 votes.

First Six Canadian Astronauts
- Marc Garneau
- Roberta Bondar
- Bjarni Tryggavason
- Bob Thirsk
- Chris Hadfield
- Steven Maclean

native icons

Who was Hiawatha?

The legendary Hiawatha may have been an actual person — a leader of vision, and the architect of the Iroquois Confederacy in pre-Columbian North America. He was allegedly a gifted orator who convinced the Mohawk, Seneca, Cayuga, Onondaga, and Oneida nations to unite. The Tuscaroras joined the Confederacy later, making it the Six Nations.

How did Chief Matonabbee contribute to Canadian exploration?

Quickies
Did you know ...
- that in 1940 a Hollywood studio planned to make a movie based on the legend of the historical Hiawatha? The idea was scrapped due to concerns that Hiawatha's message of peace could be perceived as communist propaganda.

The epic trek across the Arctic barren grounds made by English explorer Samuel Hearne from December 1770 to June 1772 would not have been possible without the help of the Dene Chief Matonabbee. A previous Native guide had abandoned Hearne in the middle of nowhere, and the explorer probably would have perished if Matonabbee had not come along. In the time that Hearne spent travelling with Matonabbee's people, he learned valuable lessons about Arctic survival, and collected important geographic and scientific information.

How was Joseph Brant a man of two worlds?

Joseph Brant (Thayendanega) was a hereditary Mohawk chief. He was also the protégé of Sir William Johnson, the British Superintendent of Indian Affairs in the colony of New York. Johnson, who was married to Joseph's sister Molly, provided young Brant with a sound education. While the teenaged Brant was learning classical literature, he was also fighting alongside fellow warriors against the French in the Seven Years War. In 1763, Brant sided with the British against the

Ottawa Chief Pontiac. By the time of the American Revolution, Brant was secretary for Sir John Johnson, Sir William's son. Brant was an influential leader who convinced most of the chiefs of the Iroquois Confederacy to support the British during the war, and he proved himself to be a skilled military tactician. Following the British defeat, he led his people to a new home on the banks of the Grand River in Upper Canada. There he encouraged them to make the transition from their traditional ways to a European agricultural lifestyle. The city of Brantford is named after him.

Why is the Shawnee Chief Tecumseh considered a Canadian hero?

Tecumseh was a visionary who believed that the only way the Native people could resist American expansion was for them to unite. For most of his adult life Tecumseh tried to forge an Indian Confederacy. That dream seemed all but shattered with the American victory at the Battle of Tippecanoe in 1811. However, when war broke out between the British and the Americans in 1812, Tecumseh saw an opportunity to establish his Confederacy with British help. Tecumseh was especially impressed with General Isaac Brock, who seemed to be made of tougher stuff than other British officers he had met. Without Tecumseh's assistance, Brock would not have been able to pull off his spectacular victory at Detroit, and Upper Canada would have been wide open for invasion. Unfortunately, Brock was killed a few months later. In 1814, at the Battle of Moraviantown, Tecumseh died fighting in defence of Upper Canada, ending forever the hope of an Indian Confederacy.

What renowned warrior chief never went to war against white expansion in the Canadian West?

The Cree Chief Piapot (born about 1816), earned fame and honour as a young warrior, and later in life he was certainly opposed to the coming of the railroads and the signing away of Cree territory. But he believed armed resistance to the whites was futile. He took no part in the Red River Rebellion of 1869 or the Northwest Rebellion of 1885. However, Piapot refused to be assimilated into white culture. He did not convert to Christianity, and he encouraged his people to hold to their traditional beliefs and ceremonies. By the time Piapot died in 1908, he was a revered figure among the Natives of the Canadian prairies, and is still honoured as a defender of First Nations culture.

Quickies
Did you know ...

- Piapot refused to forbid his people to stage rain dances, which the Canadian government considered pagan and unacceptable, so Ottawa officially deposed him as chief in 1899? His people would not select a replacement, and Piapot remained chief — unofficially — for the rest of his life.

How was Poundmaker both a peacemaker and a warrior?

In the early 1870s, the Cree Chief Poundmaker (Pitikwahanapiwiyin) was instrumental in ending the generations-long war between the Cree and Blackfoot nations. To formalize the peace agreement he became the adopted son — at age 47 — of the Blackfoot Chief Crowfoot. However, Poundmaker remained a focus of the discontent the Cree people felt over mistreatment by the Canadian government. In 1885, he and his warriors joined Gabriel Dumont and the Métis in the Northwest Rebellion. Poundmaker knew they could not win the war, but he hoped to draw government attention to the desperate situation of the Cree and other prairie nations. Poundmaker defeated a Canadian military force at the Battle of Cut Knife Hill. A month later he voluntarily surrendered to Major General Frederick Middleton. At his trial, Poundmaker said, "You did not catch me. I gave myself up." Poundmaker was sentenced to three years in prison, but was released after six months because he had tuberculosis. He died on July 4, 1886.

Why is the Cree Chief Big Bear looked upon as a tragic figure?

In the 1870s, Big Bear refused to sign any treaties with the Canadian government, considering them to be unfair to the Native peoples of the prairies. He tried to encourage other Native leaders to insist that reserve lands for the various indigenous nations be next to each other so there would be a large First Nations confederacy within Canada. However, the Canadian government would not agree to this. Starvation resulting from the disappearance of the buffalo finally forced Big Bear to take his people to a reserve and accept meagre government handouts. The whites still considered him a troublemaker. In the Northwest Rebellion of 1885, Big Bear opposed violence but was unable to prevent young warriors from following the war chief Wandering Spirit. These warriors massacred nine people at Frog Lake. After a Canadian army crushed the rebellion at the Battle of Batoche, Big Bear was one of the Native leaders who was tracked down and arrested. Even though he was not responsible for any of the violence, he was sentenced to three years in prison. He was released early due to poor health, and died on January 17, 1888, at the age of 62.

Quickies

Did you know ...

- that when the governor general of Canada, the Marquis of Lorne, visited the West in 1881, authorities chose Poundmaker to be his guide, partly because of the chief's handsome looks and aristocratic bearing?

What Blackfoot chief was best noted for his statesmanship and diplomacy?

Crowfoot was not a hereditary chief, but his courage in war and his perception in dealings with the whites and with traditional enemies like the Crow, the Cree, and the Sioux revealed him as a natural leader. As a youth Crowfoot was in 19 battles with rival tribes, and was wounded six times. One of his most heroic deeds was to kill a grizzly bear with a lance. As an adult, Crowfoot rarely took the warpath, preferring negotiation and compromise. He adopted the Cree Chief Poundmaker and befriended the traders of the Hudson's Bay Company. Crowfoot deplored the whiskey trade that was so ruinous to the Native peoples, and he welcomed the arrival of the North West Mounted Police. Crowfoot became disillusioned with the Canadian government, but he had visited cities like Regina and Winnipeg and realized that armed opposition to the whites would be futile. He did not join the Northwest Rebellion of 1885. Crowfoot died of tuberculosis in 1890.

Why did Simon Gun-an-noot run from the law for 13 years?

Simon Gun-an-noot was a member of the Kispiox Clan of the Carrier Nation, and operated a successful ranch near New Hazelton, British Columbia. In June 1906, two white men, Alex McIntosh and Max Leclair, were found murdered. Both had been shot in the back. Hours earlier Simon Gun-an-noot had been involved in a violent quarrel with McIntosh, and so was immediately suspected, though there was no evidence connecting him with the murders. Gun-an-noot did not think he would get a fair trial in a white court, so he fled into the mountains, taking his whole family with him. For 13 years Gun-an-noot evaded every attempt to catch him, even making the much-vaunted Pinkerton Detective Agency look foolish. He became a legend among the Native people, none of whom tried to collect the reward on Gun-an-noot's head by informing on him or helping the white posses. In June 1919, after friends had secured him the services of a well-respected lawyer, Gun-an-noot voluntarily surrendered to the police. At his trial the jury took only 15 minutes to reach a verdict of not guilty.

How did Tom Longboat astound the world in 1907?

Tom Longboat was an Onondaga from the Six Nations Reserve near Brantford, Ontario. In 1907 he became the first Native long distance runner to win the Boston Marathon. He ran the 24-and-a-half-mile course in a record breaking 2:24:24. He had beaten the previous record by an incredible four minutes and 59 seconds. The following year Longboat collapsed during the Olympic marathon. Nonetheless, he went on to have a distinguished professional career as a runner.

Quickies

Did you know ...

- that in spite of his athletic accomplishments, Tom Longboat often experienced the ugliness of racism? He was frequently subjected to racial smears in the press. When his running career ended, he worked as a street cleaner in Toronto.

Who was the first "Treaty Indian" to be elected to a Canadian provincial legislature?

In 1981, Elijah Harper, a Cree from Red Sucker Lake, Manitoba, won the provincial riding of Rupertsland for the New Democratic Party, making him the first "Treaty Indian" to sit in a provincial legislature. In 1990, Harper gained national attention, and admiration, when he voted no to the controversial Meech Lake Accord, which he said ignored the rights of Native peoples. Harper's opposition, coupled with that of Newfoundland Premier Clyde Wells, effectively killed the Meech Lake Accord.

**paragons
of politics**

Who were the Baldwins of Upper Canada?

William Warren Baldwin, a doctor and lawyer in Toronto, was a Reformer who opposed the elitist, ultra-conservative rule of the Family Compact, but did not agree with William Lyon Mackenzie's idea of bringing an American form of republican government to Canada. He firmly believed in the British parliamentary system, and he rejected Mackenzie's call for armed rebellion. In 1835, Baldwin was one of the founders of the Constitutional Reform Society. In 1848, William Baldwin's son Robert joined the French Canadian Reform advocate Hippolyte La Fontaine to lead the Great Ministry which won the struggle for responsible government in 1849. The Baldwins and La Fontaine were true pioneers of Canadian independence.

Who was Canada's poet-politician?

Quickies

Did you know ...

- English novelist Charles Dickens, lifelong champion of the common people, visited Canada in 1842 and described the supporters of the Family Compact as adherents of "rabid Toryism"?

Louis-Honoré Fréchette, born in 1839, was a poet, lawyer, and journalist who courageously attacked the power of the Roman Catholic Church in Quebec. The Church responded by discouraging potential clients from taking their legal business to Fréchette. He left Quebec in 1865 to spend six years in exile in the United States. He returned in 1871, and in 1874 was elected to the House of Commons. Fréchette lost his seat in the election of 1878. He now devoted all of his time and energy to writing, and in 1881 his fourth book of poetry, *Les Fleurs Boreales*, was awarded the Prix Montoyon by the Acadamie Francaise. Fréchette followed this with the work that is considered his masterpiece, *La Legende d'un Peuple*, published in 1887. This epic poem celebrated the heroes of French Canada before the British Conquest. It is now considered the first major Canadian poem in either English or French. *La Legende* was seen by Fréchette's contemporaries as a magnificent patriotic work. Because of it he was given sinecure at the Legislative Council. Fréchette went on to write poems, plays, essays, and histories that established him as one of Canada's literary pioneers.

How did Egerton Ryerson revolutionize education in Canada?

Compulsory, free education for all children was unheard of in early colonial Canada. Schools were privately run institutions for the children of the privileged, or they were run by churches. Egerton Ryerson believed that education should be secular, and should be available for children of all social classes. He travelled all over Europe and the United States studying various methods of schooling. Ryerson was strongly opposed by Upper Canada's Family Compact and the powerful Anglican Church. Nonetheless, in 1844, Ryerson was made Chief Superintendent of Education for Canada West. From that post he fought long and hard to get government funding for schools, and for a college to train teachers. He was a pioneer in recruiting women as teachers, which was considered a male occupation. His greatest achievement was the Ontario School Act of 1871, which guaranteed universal education.

Why were Canada's Fathers of Confederation heroes?

The decades between the American Revolution and the American Civil War were uncertain times for the colonies of British North America. In the War of 1812 they defeated American invaders, but that did not guarantee security or lead to unity. Rebellions in Upper and Lower Canada, greater opportunities for immigrants in the United States, and a general lack of unifying bonds among the British colonies did not bode well for confederation. The men who became the Fathers of Confederation had to look past regional politics, petty bickering, and French-English differences to see a greater good. It was not until the final year of the American Civil War, when it seemed entirely possible that a victorious Union army might turn its attention to Canada once the Southern Confederacy had been defeated, that the idea of a united British North America started to gain popular support. Even then, some voices favoured joining the United States and others insisted on remaining under the colonial administration of Mother England. Canadian Confederation had strong opponents, and the men who favoured it faced an uphill battle.

How did the American Civil War help to galvanize the Fathers of Confederation into action?

During the Civil War, Britain did not formally recognize the Confederate government in Richmond, Virginia, but clearly favoured the South. The British continued to do business with the South, and built warships for the Confederate navy. Confederate spies and raiders used Canada as a base from which to mount operations against the North. Sea captains from the Maritimes regularly ran the United States Navy's blockade to deliver supplies to Southern ports. All this had many people in the North, including some top generals, clamouring for an invasion of Canada. The Fathers of Confederation realized that only by forming a strong union could they hope to avoid American annexation.

Who were the leading Fathers of Confederation?

John A. Macdonald was unarguably the driving force behind Confederation, and is still regarded as one of Canada's greatest prime ministers. However, he would not have realized his dream of a Canadian nation had it not been for the efforts of six other men: Thomas D'Arcy McGee of Montreal, one of the most eloquent orators of the time; George Brown of Canada West (Ontario), founder of the *Globe* newspaper; Georges-Étienne Cartier, political leader of Canada East (Quebec) who believed a united Canada was in the best interests of the Quebecois; Alexander T. Galt, who represented Anglophones in Canada East; Samuel L. Tilley, the premier of New Brunswick; and Charles Tupper, the premier of Nova Scotia.

Who were the other Fathers of Confederation?

Besides the names already mentioned, the following are considered Fathers of Confederation for the original four provinces that made up Canada in 1867:

Nova Scotia
- Adams George Archibald
- Robert B. Dickey
- William Alexander Henry
- Jonathan McCully
- John William Richie

New Brunswick
- Edward Barron Chandler
- Charles Fisher
- John Hamilton Gray
- John Mercer Johnson
- Peter Mitchell
- William H. Steeves
- Robert Duncan Wilmot

Quebec
- Jean-Charles Chapais
- Hector-Louis Langevin
- Étienne-Paschal Taché

Ontario
- Alexander Campbell
- James Cockburn
- William Pearce Howland
- William McDougall
- Oliver Mowat

Why is Sir Wilfrid Laurier considered one of Canada's greatest prime ministers?

Laurier, a Liberal, was Canada's first francophone prime minister. He holds the record for the most consecutive federal elections won (4), and his 15 years as prime minister is the longest unbroken term in that office. His nearly 45 years of public service in the House of Commons is also a record, and no other Canadian politician has served as long (31 years, 8 months) as leader of a major political party. Canada expanded under Laurier's tenure, and he was known for his policies of conciliation and compromise between English and French Canada. He was a strong advocate of a French-English partnership in Canada.

Why was Lester Pearson awarded the Nobel Prize?

In 1956, Lester Pearson was Minister of Foreign Affairs in the government of Prime Minister Louis St. Laurent. When the Suez Crisis threatened to embroil France, the United Kingdom, Egypt, and Israel in war, Pearson defused the potential international disaster and created the United Nations Emergency Force to police the disputed area. For this, Pearson was awarded the 1957 Nobel Peace Prize. Pearson is considered the father of the modern concept of peacekeeping. Pearson was Prime Minister of Canada from April 22, 1963, to April 20, 1968.

Twelve Other Men Considered to be Fathers of Confederation

- Louis Riel — brought Manitoba into Confederation in 1870.
- Armour De Cosmo — brought British Columbia into Confederation in 1871.
- George Coles, John Hamilton Gray (not to be confused with the man of the same name from New Brunswick), Thomas Heath Haviland, Andrew Archibald Macdonald, Edward Palmer, William Henry Pope, and Edward Whelan — brought Prince Edward Island into Confederation in 1873.
- Frederick Carter and Ambrose Shea of Newfoundland — considered Fathers of Confederation even though Newfoundland initially rejected Confederation.
- Joseph Roberts Smallwood — brought Newfoundland and Labrador into Confederation in 1949.

How did Lincoln Alexander make Canadian history?

In 1968, Lincoln Alexander, representing the Ontario riding of Hamilton West, became Canada's first Black member of Parliament. In 1985, Alexander was appointed lieutenant-governor of Ontario, making him the first Black person in Canada to serve in a viceregal position. Lincoln

Alexander has been awarded the Order of Ontario and has been named a Companion of the Order of Canada.

Quickies
Did you know ...
• the Lincoln M. Alexander Parkway in Hamilton was named in Alexander's honour? Ironically, he has never had a driver's licence.

Who was the first Black woman to run for the leadership of a Canadian national political party?

Rosemary Brown was born in Jamaica in 1930. When she came to Canada in 1950 to attend university, she encountered racism. White students did not want her for a roommate, and she had difficulty finding employment. She was determined to change things, and in 1972 she became the first Black woman elected to the British Columbia legislature. Two years later, the New Democratic Party asked her to run for the party's leadership. She did not win, but the fact that she was in the race helped raise public awareness of the potential for both women and Blacks in politics. She continued to work for human rights, women's issues, and world peace. Rosemary Brown died in 2003.

Quickies
Did you know ...
• Rosemary Brown once said, "To be Black and female in a society which is both racist and sexist is to be in the unique position of having nowhere to go but up"?

Who was the first Black woman elected to Canada's Parliament?

In 1993, Jean Augustine, representing the Ontario riding of Etobicoke-Lakeshore became the first black woman elected to Parliament. She served as parliamentary secretary to Prime Minister Jean Chretien 1994 to 1996. In 2004, she became the first Black woman to occupy the Speaker's Chair in the Canadian House of Commons. Jean Augustine has received the YWCA Woman of Distinction Award, the Kaye Livingston Award, the Ontario Volunteer Award, the Pride Newspaper Achievement Award, the Toronto Lion's Club Onyx Award, and the Rubena Willis Special Recognition Award.

canada's rebels

Who was the forgotten hero of political reform in Upper Canada?

Twenty years before the Mackenzie Rebellion, a Scot named Robert Fleming Gourlay wanted to encourage immigration to Upper Canada. He learned that the two greatest obstacles to settlement were the ruling Family Compact and the Church of England, who reserved huge tracts of the best land for themselves. Gourlay called this "paltry patronage and ruinous favouritism." In 1818 he organized a convention at York (Toronto) to petition reforms from the new governor, Sir Peregrine Maitland. It was an orderly meeting attended by only 14 men, but the Family Compact saw Gourley as a serious threat. They came down on him with all their might. Future conventions were banned. Gourlay was assaulted on several occasions. Anyone associated with him was blacklisted. Finally Gourlay was arrested and banished from Upper Canada. His name later became a rallying cry for the Reform Movement, though Gourlay opposed the idea of armed rebellion. Gourlay is now a largely forgotten Canadian hero, but there is a bust of him in a Toronto park.

Why did a rebellion flare up in Lower Canada (Quebec) in 1837?

The colonial government in Quebec City was controlled by a small, elitist group of men, both French and English, who jealously guarded their power and privilege. Their main political opponent, the reformist Parti Canadien (later called the Parti Patriote) called them the Château Clique. When the Château Clique not only blocked measures proposed by the Parti Patriote, but also went as far as to have members of that party arrested, the more radical reformers resorted to armed insurrection.

Who was Louis Joseph Papineau?

Louis Joseph Papineau has been called the leader of the Rebellion of 1838, though he took no part in the fighting and actually abhorred violence. In fact, he fled to the United States to avoid arrest before the bullets even began to fly, and stayed there until granted amnesty. He was a political rebel who has been perceived as an early champion of Quebec independence because he opposed British rule. He remains one of the most enigmatic hero figures in Canadian history.

What were some of the puzzling contradictions about Louis Joseph Papineau?

Papineau was conservative in theory, but revolutionary in practice. He supported political reform, but he opposed responsible government and democracy. He wanted a republican Quebec, but only if it was ruled by landed gentry like himself. He did not like English aristocrats, but he believed the *habitants* of Quebec should be subservient to a French aristocracy. At times he felt that Quebec should join the United States.

Who were Wolfred Nelson and Thomas Storrow Brown?

Nelson and Brown were both sons of Loyalist parents, but took the side of the Patriotes in demanding social and political reforms in Lower Canada. They were initially moderates, but they eventually supported armed revolution and the installation of a republican form of government modelled after that of the United States. Nelson fought against British troops at Saint-Denis. Brown lost the use of one eye in a political street fight in Montreal, and fought British troops at Saint-Charles. When the revolt was crushed, Brown fled to the United States where he remained until he was granted amnesty in 1844.

> **Quickies**
> *Did you know ...*
> - many English and Irish residents of Lower Canada supported the French-speaking Patriotes in their demand for an end to the rule of the Château Clique? On the other hand, a large number of French Canadians who opposed the Château Clique also opposed the idea of armed revolt. The Patriotes called them *vendus* (people who had sold out) and *Chouayens* (after French militiamen who had deserted during the Battle of Chougen in 1756). Harassment at the hands of Patriotes drove some *vendus* to fight alongside the British.

Nelson was arrested and exiled to Bermuda. He, too, was granted amnesty in 1844. From 1854 until 1856 Wolfred Nelson was mayor of Montreal.

Why did the death of Lieutenant George "Jock" Weir have tragic consequences for the people of Saint-Eustache?

Young Lieutenant Weir became lost while carrying dispatches to Colonel Charles Gore of the British army. He was captured by French Canadian rebels who told him he would receive fair treatment as long as he did not try to escape. Weir promised he would not try to escape, and then at the first opportunity, he made a run for it. He was re-captured and then brutally executed. Weir was shot twice, beaten with gun butts, and repeatedly stabbed and slashed with knives or sabers. Three fingers were cut off one of his hands. When the English soldiers found Weir's mutilated body, they swore they'd have revenge on the "murdering French."

What happened at Saint-Eustache?

On December 14, 1837, General John Colborne led an army of about 2,000 British troops and Canadian militia against Saint-Eustache, which was a rebel stronghold. The Patriote leader in the town was Jean-Olivier Chenier, a doctor and politician who had become a follower of Papineau. Most of his army of 1,500 men fled when British artillery began to bombard the town, but Chenier and about 80 others holed up in the stone church. The British gained access to the ground floor of the building, but couldn't dislodge Chenier and his men from the choir loft and the upper chambers, so they set the interior on fire. Then they surrounded the building and waited with guns and bayonets. The word passed from soldier to soldier, "Remember Jock Weir." Some of the rebels died in the flames. Those who tried to escape were shot or bayoneted. Chenier climbed out a window and was shot through the heart. Later his body was disembowelled. Vengeful soldiers ignored officers who tried to stop the slaughter, and killed men who were on their knees with their hands in the air. The revolt in Lower Canada was crushed, but Jean-Olivier Chenier and his men are remembered as martyrs. There is a statue of Chenier in Saint-Eustache.

Who was the leader of the Rebellion in Upper Canada?

The leader of the Upper Canada Rebellion of 1837–38 was William Lyon Mackenzie, a fiery Scot who was a Reform politician and a journalist. Mackenzie founded a newspaper, the *Colonial Advocate,* in which he attacked the ruling elite, known as the Family Compact. Like the Château Clique in Quebec, the Family Compact was a tightly knit group of wealthy, influential men who dominated colonial affairs and ruthlessly crushed any threat to their power.

How did the Family Compact respond to Mackenzie's attacks in the *Colonial Advocate?*

A group of young men disguised as "Indians" broke into Mackenzie's office in York in broad daylight. They smashed his printing press and threw trays of type into the harbour. Magistrates friendly to the Family Compact initially refused to prosecute the perpetrators, but Mackenzie eventually successfully sued for damages.

Why did Mackenzie turn to armed insurrection?

Mackenzie was elected to the assembly of Upper Canada, but on several occasions he was ejected for speaking against the Family Compact and institutions like the Bank of Upper Canada. He travelled to Britain in hope of drawing attention to the need for political reform in Upper Canada, but was ignored. Mackenzie lost faith in the British parliamentary system, and began to speak in favour of the American republican system. In an election in 1836, Sir Francis Bond Head, the lieutenant-governor of

143

Upper Canada, actively campaigned for the Family Compact, denouncing Reformers like Mackenzie as traitors. Mackenzie lost his seat in the Assembly, and looked to other means to bring about change.

How did the Rebellion in Lower Canada influence Mackenzie's plan of action?

Almost all of the British troops garrisoned in Upper Canada had been sent to Lower Canada to put down the insurrection there. Mackenzie thought that with the redcoats gone, the time was right to strike and seize the government in York.

Where did the main engagement of the Mackenzie Rebellion take place?

On December 7, 1837, Mackenzie's ragtag army of about 500 poorly armed rebels met a force of about 1,000 militia led by the War of 1812 hero James Fitzgibbon at Montgomery's Tavern, about three and a half miles north of Toronto. There was an exchange of gunfire, and then the rebels turned and fled. One rebel was killed and several were wounded. The militia had five or six men wounded. The "battle" of Montgomery's Tavern lasted only a few minutes.

What was the aftermath of the Mackenzie rebellion?

Two of Mackenzie's followers, Samuel Lount and Peter Matthews, were hanged. About a hundred more were shipped off to a penal colony in Australia. Mackenzie fled to the United States and set up a "republic" on Navy Island in the Niagara River. He was arrested by the Americans and served a year in jail for breach of neutrality laws. For four years he was a political journalist for a New York newspaper. Mackenzie later expressed great disappointment in the American system of government. He said that if he had actually seen it at work sooner, he would never have led a rebellion. Mackenzie was eventually pardoned and returned to Toronto. By this time the Canadian colonies had responsible government and the power of the Family Compact was broken. Mackenzie served in the legislature until 1858. He died in 1861. Mackenzie's house at 82 Bond Street in Toronto is now a museum.

> **Quickies**
> *Did you know ...*
> • Prime Minister William Lyon Mackenzie King was a grandson of William Lyon Mackenzie?

Why is Louis Riel considered the founder of Manitoba?

Born in the Red River Settlement in 1844, Louis Riel was educated in Montreal and rose to leadership among the Métis even though he had only one-eighth Native blood. Riel was eloquent, deeply religious, charismatic, and ambitious. When Canadian government surveyors arrived on Métis land in 1869, Riel sent them packing. In what has been called the Red River Rebellion, Riel and his followers took possession of Fort Garry (Winnipeg). Riel formed a provisional government and drew up a "List of Rights" which was submitted to Ottawa. After much debate and political bargaining, this resulted in the passing of the Manitoba Act and the creation of a new province, which Riel himself named.

Why did Riel have to flee from Manitoba?

When Riel seized Fort Garry, the Canadian government sent out a military force under Colonel Garnet Wolseley to assert federal authority. Riel had to flee to avoid arrest on a charge of murder. There were even rumours that Ontario militiamen with Wolseley intended to lynch him.

Who was Riel charged with killing?

Among the new settlers in the Red River country were a number of people from Ontario who were also members of the Protestant Orange Lodge.

The Orangemen, who wielded considerable political clout in Ontario, were strongly anti-French and anti-Catholic, and were openly contemptuous of Riel and the Métis. One of the most troublesome was a ruffian named Thomas Scott, who repeatedly defied Riel's provisional government. Riel had Scott arrested on charges of interfering with the government. Scott was tried and sentenced to death. Ignoring advisors who wanted the death sentence commuted, Riel had Scott shot by a firing squad. In life, Scott had been a bully and a boor, but in death he achieved the status of martyr in Orange Ontario. His execution was the greatest blunder in Riel's career.

What happened to Riel after the Red River Rebellion?

Riel was elected to Parliament, but was unable to take his seat. Prime Minister Alexander Mackenzie granted Riel amnesty, on the condition that Riel accept banishment from Canada for five years. He went to the United States, became an American citizen, and eventually became a schoolteacher in Montana.

Why did Riel return to Canada?

In the summer of 1884, a deputation of Métis from what is now Saskatchewan went to Montana to seek Riel's help. Once again they were experiencing difficulties with a Canadian government that cared little about their rights and needs. The Métis thought that Riel was the only man who could effectively represent them. The leader of the deputation that went to Montana was Gabriel Dumont.

What qualities of leadership did Gabriel Dumont possess?

Born in the Red River country in 1837, Gabriel Dumont had the physical skills and the personal traits that made him a natural leader of the Métis people. He was a renowned buffalo hunter, as skilled with a bow and arrow as he was with a rifle. He was an excellent horseman and tracker. While still a boy, he proved his courage and fighting ability in a battle with the Sioux. Besides French, he spoke six Native languages fluently. Dumont was a compassionate man who shared his meat from the buffalo hunt with people in need. As a young man he realized that the Métis and the Native peoples had a common foe in the whites who were moving onto the prairies, and he was instrumental in making peace with long time enemies of the Métis like the Sioux and the Blackfoot. As the great herds of buffalo dwindled, Dumont helped convince the Métis to turn to farming.

When was Gabriel Dumont president of a "republic"?

In 1873, the Métis gathered at St. Laurent on the South Saskatchewan River and formed what was in effect an autonomous little republic. They drew up laws and elected a council with Dumont as president. Dumont was illiterate, but for two years he and his council governed with fairness and common sense. They passed legislation to deal with land and timber rights, and to conserve the buffalo. Dumont's unique prairie government was dissolved in 1875 with the arrival of the North West Mounted Police.

How did Riel's return to Canada lead to rebellion?

Riel wrote to Ottawa, outlining the needs and grievances of the Métis people. The government ignored the letter. Riel, who by this time was clearly mentally unstable, decided that he had a mission from God to be the messiah for the Métis. He declared the Métis community of Batoche to be the capital of a new nation, ruled by him, and the centre of a new church, with Riel as its head. Riel sent messengers to Native leaders like Big Bear and Poundmaker, urging them to join him in a revolt against the Canadian government. Ottawa responded by sending an army to the west.

Where did the main battle of the Northwest Rebellion take place?

There were numerous skirmishes, but the biggest clash between Gabriel Dumont's tough Métis fighters and Major General Frederick Middleton's army took place at Batoche in May of 1885. There were 800 Canadian troops against no more than 200 Métis, but Dumont's men gave the Canadians all they could handle. Not until the Métis were practically out of ammunition were the red-coated soldiers able to effectively press home an attack and route them.

What happened to Dumont and Riel?

Dumont fled to the United States, where he lived until he was granted amnesty. Riel surrendered and was charged with high treason. He was tried by an all-English, all-Protestant jury and found guilty. Though there were those who believed Riel was insane, government-appointed doctors said he was a reasonable and accountable person who knew the difference between right and wrong. Riel was hanged in Regina on November 16, 1885. The St. Boniface, Manitoba, Museum has the moccasins and face mask Riel wore at his execution.

Why does Riel remain a controversial figure?

To many people Riel was a heroic figure who stood up for the rights of the Métis, who were certainly being mistreated by the federal government. In Quebec, Riel has been wrapped in a cloak of martyrdom that not even Louis Joseph Papineau achieved. However, others point out that, as obnoxious a character as Thomas Scott was, Riel had no legal right to have him executed. They believe Riel was insane by the time he led the Northwest Rebellion, and should have been committed to an institution.

champions of sport

How did Tommy Burns become the first Canadian heavyweight boxing champion of the world?

Tommy Burns (born Noah Brusso in Normandy Township, Ontario, June 17, 1889) was an up and coming middleweight boxer in 1905, anxious for a shot at the middleweight title. Marvin Hart inherited the world heavyweight title when champion James Jeffries retired from the ring. Hart was obliged to defend his new title, and chose Burns as his first challenger, expecting an easy victory. At five-foot-seven, and 175 pounds, Burns was considered too small to be classed as a heavyweight contender. Nonetheless, he won a decision over Hart in a 20-round bout in Los Angeles on February 23, 1906. In a period of less than two years, Burns successfully defended his title 11 times, always against much bigger opponents, and usually winning by knockout. In San Diego he took on two challengers in one night, and knocked both out in the first round. Burns defended his title in the United States, Great Britain, France, and Australia.

Quickies
Did you know ...

- that it galled white America that a Black boxer had become heavyweight champion, and American sports writers did everything they could to downplay Jack Johnson's accomplishment? One tactic was to diminish the ability of the man he had beaten. As a result, Tommy Burns's reputation suffered. Only many years later would sports historians admit that Burns, the only Canadian-born heavyweight champion, was a courageous David against Johnson's Goliath, and on that occasion Goliath won.

Where did Tommy Burns lose the world heavyweight championship?

In Sydney, Australia, Burns defeated the hometown favourite Bill Squires, and then made boxing history when he agreed to fight the Black American challenger Jack Johnson. Previously, no white champion would get into the ring with a black boxer. The bout was held on December 26, 1908. Standing over six feet tall, and weighing in at 203 pounds, Johnson dwarfed Burns. He had a long reach that Burns could not penetrate. It was rumoured that Burns had been sick with jaundice or influenza, and was 15 pounds under his normal fighting rate. Burns endured 14 punishing rounds until police stopped the fight and Johnson was declared the winner — the first Black world heavyweight champion.

How did George Chuvalo restore legitimacy to professional boxing?

In 1966, professional boxing was reeling from several body blows. Muhammad Ali (Cassius Clay) had won a pair of controversial victories over Sonny Liston, and there were accusations that the fights had been fixed. The American Legion, incensed over Ali's refusal to be inducted into the military on the grounds of being a conscientious objector, threatened to boycott any American city that hosted an Ali fight. Ernie Terrell, with whom Ali was scheduled to have his next bout, backed out. Ali was offered a bout in Toronto with George Chuvalo, the heavyweight champion of Canada. Boxing fans anticipated an easy victory for Ali, who up to that point had been winning all of his fights by knockout or TKO. Instead, Ali found himself in a hard battle with an opponent who just wouldn't go down. Ali won the match by decision, but later said that Chuvalo was the toughest opponent he had ever faced. Chuvalo's gutsy performance earned him, and professional boxing, a whole new respect.

Who was "The man with the burning eyes"?

Maurice "Rocket" Richard, superstar forward with the Montreal Canadiens from 1942 to 1960, played the game of hockey with such intensity, other players said he appeared to have "burning eyes." Richard was the first player to score 50 goals in a season, and he did it in just 50 games. He was also the first player to score 500 goals in his career. His record-setting five-goal game against the Toronto Maple Leafs in the 1944 Stanley Cup semi-finals is considered one of the great moments in Canadian professional sports. At the end of the game Richard was selected as first, second, and third star.

What was the only NHL team to come back from a 3–0 game deficit to win the Stanley Cup?

The Toronto Maple Leafs did it in 1942. In the Cup final series against the Detroit Red Wings, the Leafs lost the first three games but then stormed back to win the next three and tie the series. In front of a record-breaking crowd at Maple Leaf Gardens the home-town heroes won game seven and the Stanley Cup.

Who was the hero of the 1972 Summit Series?

The eight-game Summit Series, held in September of 1972, was the first competition between full-strength Soviet and Canadian national ice hockey teams. Canada won the series four games to three, with one game ending in a tie. The winning goals in games six, seven, and eight were all scored by Paul Henderson. The final game of the series was watched by more people in Canada — about 16 million — than any other televised show before or since. Henderson's winning goal in game eight, scored with just 34 seconds left in the third period, is considered the greatest moment in hockey history.

In 1997, on the 25th anniversary of the goal, Paul was immortalized on a postage stamp issued by Canada Post and a silver coin by The Royal Canadian Mint.

What is a "Gordie Howe hat-trick"?

Gordie Howe was one of the professional hockey's leading stars from 1946 until 1980. In the era before Wayne Gretzky he held more scoring records than any other player. Howe was a prolific goal scorer and a brilliant play maker. He was also known for his tough, aggressive style of play. When a player scores three goals in a game, it is called a hat-trick. When a player scores a goal, assists on another player's goal, and is involved in a fight all in the same game, he is said to have had a "Gordie Howe hat-trick."

What was Bobby Orr's most dramatic goal?

Undoubtedly Orr's most memorable goal was the 1970 Stanley Cup winner he scored against St. Louis Blues goaltender Glenn Hall. Just as Orr took his shot, he was tripped by Blues defenceman Noel Picard. Orr was flying through the air as the puck went into the net. The photograph of the airborne Orr is one of the most famous hockey pictures ever taken.

How did Darryl Sittler electrify Toronto hockey fans on February 7, 1976?

That night, playing on a line with Lanny MacDonald and Errol Thompson, Toronto Maple Leafs star Darryl Sittler racked up a record-breaking 10 points; six goals and four assists. It is an NHL record that still stands. The victim was the Boston Bruins' back-up goaltender Dave Reece. Toronto won the game 11–4.

How many NHL records did Wayne Gretzky achieve?

At the time of his retirement, Wayne Gretzky held or shared in 61 NHL scoring records, including most regular season goals (894), most regular season assists (1,963), most goals in a single regular season (92), and the fasted 50 goals (39 games).

Who is the Canadian Football League's pass king?

On October 28, 2000, Damon Allen of the B.C. Lions made a 45-yard touchdown

Fifteen Canadian Hockey Heroes and Their Nicknames

- Maurice Richard — the Rocket
- Henri Richard — the Pocket-Rocket
- Wayne Gretzky — the Great One
- Mario Lemieux — the Magnificent One
- Gordie Howe — Mr. Hockey
- Bobby Hull — the Golden Jet
- Frank Mahovlich — the Big M
- Yvan Cournoyer — the Roadrunner
- Lionel Conacher — the Big Train
- Eddie Shack — the Entertainer
- Emile Francis — the Cat
- Curtis Joseph — Cujo
- Bernie Geoffrion — Boom-Boom
- Lorne Worsley — Gump
- Ted Lindsay — Terrible Ted

Five of the Greatest Moments in Canadian International Hockey History

- The 1972 Summit Series with the Soviet Union.
- The Canadian Olympic gold medal game against the United States in 2002.
- The 1987 Canada Cup final against the Soviet Union.
- The Canadian Juniors 2005 championship victory over Russia.
- The Canadian women's hockey team's gold medal victory over Sweden in the 2006 Olympics.

pass to Alfred Jackson that moved him past the legendary Russ Jackson into sole possession of first place in the CFL's all-time passing yards list. Allen went on to become the most prolific passer in professional football history.

What Canadian race car champion followed in his father's footsteps?

Gilles Villeneuve won six Formula One Grand Prix races before he was killed in an on-track accident in 1982. His son Jacques has won the CART Championship (1995), the Indianapolis 500 (1995), and the Formula One World Championship (1997).

What was the first non-U.S.-based Major League Baseball team to win the World Series?

In 1992 the Toronto Blue Jays defeated the Atlanta Braves to become the first franchise outside the United States to win a World Series championship. The Blue Jays won the championship again in 1993. They were the first back-to-back champions since the New York Yankees of 1977–78.

Who was the first Canadian-born golfer to win a professional major tournament?

In 2003, Mike Weir of Bright's Grove, Ontario, won the Masters, making him the first Canadian to win a major. During a ceremonial face-off at the Air Canada Centre in Toronto, Weir was given a minute-long

Some Canadian Sports Heroes Who Have Won Olympic Gold

- Percy William — running, 1928
- Barbara Ann Scott — figure skating, 1948
- Vic Emery, John Emery, Doug Anakin, Peter Kirby — bobsled, 1964
- Nancy Greene — downhill skiing, 1968
- Alex Bauman — swimming, 1984
- Gaeten Boucher — speed skating, 1984
- Lennox Lewis — boxing, 1988
- Kerrin Lee-Gartner — downhill skiing,1992
- Myriam Bedard — biathlon, 1994
- Kathleen Heddle, Marnie McBean — rowing, 1996
- Robert Esmie, Bruny Surin, Glenroy Gilbert, Carlton Chambers, Donovan Bailey — running, 1996
- Sandra Schmirler, Jan Betker, Marcia Gudereit, Joan McCusker, Atina Ford — curling, 1998
- Daniel Nestor, Sebastian Lareau — tennis, 2000
- Daniel Igali — wrestling, 2000
- Simon Whitfield — triathlon, 2000
- Marc Gagnon — speed skating, 2002
- Catriona Le May Doan — speed skating, 2002
- Jamie Sale, David Pelletier — pairs figure skating, 2002
- Adam Van Koeverden — canoe and kayak, 2004
- Beckie Scott — cross country skiing, 2004
- Brad Gushue, Jamie Korab, Mike Adam, Mike Nichols — curling, 2006
- Cindy Klassen and Clara Hughes — speed skating, 2006

standing ovation, making him quite likely the only golfer to be so honoured at a hockey game.

Which Paralympian was named Canadian Athlete of the Year in 2008?

In 2008, wheelchair racer Chantal Petitclerc was awarded both the Lou Marsh Trophy and Canadian Press's Bobbie Rosenfeld Award as Canada's Female Athlete of the Year. Petitclerc, who lost the use of both legs in an accident at the age of 13, had been competing in the Paralympic Games since 1992. Over five Games she had amassed an astounding 21 Paralympic medals, including five gold medals at the 2004 Summer Games in Athens. She holds world records in the 100-, 200-, 400-, 800-, and 1,500-metre distances. A truly inspirational athlete, a municipal ice hockey arena in her home town of Saint-Marc-des-Carrières now bears her name.

Which Olympian had a doll created in her image?

Barbara Ann Scott was the first Canadian woman to win an Olympic gold medal in figure skating. After her win at the 1948 Winter Olympics in St. Moritz, Switzerland, she returned home to Canada to a hero's welcome. The girl who became known as "Canada's Sweetheart" was thrown a huge civic reception, presented with a new car by the mayor of her hometown of Ottawa (which she had to return in order to retain her amateur athlete status), and honoured by the Reliable Toy Company with the creation of a Barbara Ann Scott doll. She was a great inspiration for many girls born in the late 1940s and 1950s, quite a few of whom had been named after the popular skater.

martyrs
and marchers

What legendary Prohibition-era rumrunner was also looked upon as a working class hero?

During the years of American Prohibition, Ben Kerr of Hamilton, Ontario, was known as the King of the Rumrunners for his daring escapades smuggling liquor and beer across Lake Ontario in all sorts of weather, and under the noses of the United States Coast Guard. But even before his bootlegging career, Kerr won the admiration of working class Hamiltonians because of an incident that occurred during the Hamilton Street Railway Strike of 1909. The strike had been particularly violent, and a curfew was in effect. One night some soldiers and police enforcing that curfew barged into an ice-cream parlour where Ben Kerr was entertaining patrons with a piano. The police were wielding their billy clubs and the soldiers were threatening people with bayonets. Kerr was a supporter of labour unions, and so took the side of the civilians when the intruders became rough and abusive. He felled two of them with his piano stool before he was clubbed down himself. He escaped assault charges, and emerged as a local working class hero. Kerr's disdain for danger ultimately led to his death. In February 1929, while making a liquor run on Lake Ontario, he died when his boat was crushed by ice.

Who was Canada's "Joe Hill"?

Joe Hill was a Swedish-American labour union organizer who was executed for murder in 1915. Many people believed he was framed because of his union activities. His story has inspired songs and movies. Albert "Ginger" Goodwin was a British-born coal miner who came to Canada and worked in coal mines in Nova Scotia and on Vancouver Island. He was involved in the brutal island coal strike of 1912–13. In 1917, Goodwin was elected president of the British Columbia Federation of Labour, and Secretary of the Trail Mill and Smeltermen's Union. That same year Goodwin led a strike for the eight-hour workday at the Trail, British Columbia, lead/zinc smelter. Goodwin was known as a pacifist who opposed Canada's participation in the Great War (the First World

War). He had already been examined by the conscription board, and rated as unfit for military duty because he had black lung and bad teeth. After the Trail strike, the conscription board suddenly reversed its decision and declared Goodwin fit for military service. He fled into the bush and for some months, with the help of sympathizers, evaded the police who were looking for him as a draft dodger. On July 27, 1918, Goodwin was shot and killed by a special constable of the Dominion Police near Cumberland. The officer claimed self-defence, and was exonerated without an investigation. Many people believed Goodwin had been murdered, and public anger resulted in a general strike in Vancouver on August 2, 1918; the first general strike in Canadian history. A section of highway near Cumberland was named after Ginger Goodwin.

What was the origin of Miner's Day (also called Davis Day) on Cape Breton Island?

In the tumultuous history of coal mining in Cape Breton, 1925 was one of the worst years for trouble between the British Empire Steel Corporation (BESCO) and the Cape Breton branch of the United Mine Workers of America. BESCO president Roy Mitchell Wolvin was determined to break the union. He cut off credit at company stores at places like New Waterford where there was strong union militancy. This was followed by exchanges of labour actions and company reprisals. On June 11, at Waterford Lake, there was a confrontation between demonstrating miners and mounted company police. One of the miners present was William Davis, a 38-year-old native of Gloucestershire, England. It is uncertain why the five-foot-three-inch, 150-pound Davis was there. Some say he was present to support the union cause. Others say he was looking for a son who had skipped school, or was just out to get milk for his family. Whatever his intentions, Davis was about to become a martyr. The mounted company police suddenly charged the miners with guns blazing. William Davis was shot through the heart. An official inquiry concluded that Davis had been killed by a "stray shot," and no one was ever held accountable for his death. In Cape Breton, June 11 is a day on which people remember William Davis as well as all those who have died in mine accidents. There is a Davis Square in New Waterford, and a Davis Wilderness Trail.

What happened in Estevan, Saskatchewan, on September 29, 1931?

Men and boys working in the coal mines of southeastern Saskatchewan were among the most exploited in Canada in the first decades of the twentieth century. The mines were appallingly unsafe and unhealthy. Wages were shamefully low, and the miners were expected to do numerous jobs for no pay at all. The company houses in which the miners' families lived were squalid shacks, and the company stores in which they were obliged to shop grossly overpriced the merchandise. Then the Great Depression hit and things got worse. To rescue their profits, in 1931 the mine owners cut the already pitiful wages paid to the miners. This led to labour union activity that the mine owners tried hard to suppress. The situation came to a violent head on September 29. Striking miners staged a march through coal country from Bienfait to Estevan to draw attention to their plight and win public support. The motorcade of old cars and trucks that accompanied the marchers carried their wives and children. In Estevan the unarmed strikers were confronted with Estevan town police, RCMP constables, and the local fire department. The police told the strikers to disperse. They refused. A general fight broke out when the police started arresting people. Stones were thrown, and the police began to fire their guns. When the smoke cleared, three miners lay mortally wounded. Pete Markunas, 27, and Julian Gryshko, 26, were both shot in the stomach, and Nick Nargan, 25, was shot through the heart. Eight other strikers, four bystanders, and one RCMP officer were also wounded by police bullets. In the annals of Canadian labour history the date has been known ever since as Black Tuesday, and Markunas, Gryshko, and Nargan are recognized as martyrs to the cause of workers' rights.

**marathon
men and women**

Who was Terry Fox?

Born in Winnipeg on July 28, 1958, and raised in Port Coquitlam, British Columbia, Terry Fox was a young man who lost his right leg to cancer and then captured the hearts and imaginations of Canadians and people around the world with his courageous Marathon of Hope run in 1980. To raise money for cancer research, Terry intended to run across every Canadian province, from Newfoundland to British Columbia. It was an incredible challenge for any athlete, let alone a youth with an artificial leg. The image of Terry Fox jogging along the Trans Canada Highway in his trademark half-skip style of running, with his arms working in close to his body to maintain balance, has become a Canadian icon that is still a source of inspiration.

What was Terry Fox's background as a runner?

Terry was always competitive in sports — swimming, basketball, soccer, rugby, and baseball. He had no interest in running until a school physical education teacher encouraged him to train for cross-country running. Out of respect for the teacher, Terry began to run. He found it exhausting at first, but kept it up.

How did Terry Fox lose his right leg?

On November 16, 1976, Terry hurt his right knee in a car accident. The injury didn't seem serious, but in 1977 he was diagnosed with osteogenic sarcoma, a form of bone cancer that strikes young males more often than it does females or older people. In Terry's case it started at the knee and worked its way into the muscles and tendons. At that time the only treatment for it was amputation. Terry's leg was removed several inches above the knee. He believed that the injury he'd received in the car accident weakened his knee and made it susceptible to cancer. The doctors did not agree with this, even though trauma is a suspected cause of osteogenic sarcoma.

What made Terry decide to run across Canada?

The night before his amputation, Terry's coach showed him a magazine article about an amputee who had run in the New York Marathon. That made him realize that he could overcome his disability. Later, as he was going through what he described as "sixteen months of the physically and emotionally draining ordeal of chemotherapy" he became aware of the feelings of the other patients in the cancer clinic. "There were the faces with the brave smiles, and the ones who had given up smiling ... Somewhere the hurting must stop ... and I was determined to take myself to the limit for this cause."

How did Terry prepare for his run across Canada?

Early in 1979, Terry began his training, running half a mile a day on his artificial leg. When he could do that reasonably well he began adding another half mile a week to his regimen until he was running 13.5 miles a day. He secured assistance from the Canadian Cancer Society and several corporate sponsors for gas, a vehicle, running shoes, and money. He also received grants to buy a running leg.

When did Terry begin his run?

On April 12, 1980, Terry dipped his leg into the harbour of St. John's, Newfoundland. He filled two bottles with water from the Atlantic Ocean. He intended to keep one as a souvenir, and pour the other one into the Pacific Ocean when he dipped his leg into the harbour of Victoria, British Columbia, at the end of his cross-Canada run. He then set out to do what most people considered impossible.

How well publicized was Terry's run?

At first not many people were aware of it. But as the days passed and Terry made his way across Newfoundland and through the Maritime provinces, the media began to pay more attention, and the crowds waiting along the highway to watch Terry pass by grew significantly. By the time Terry reached Toronto his name was a household word. Thousands of people jammed Nathan Phillips Square in front of Toronto City Hall to see the young hero. Hockey great Darryl Sittler was on hand to give Terry his NHL All Star team sweater. TV star Lee Majors commented that Terry Fox was the "real" Six Million Dollar Man. At a performance in Kitchener, Ontario, Kris Kristofferson dedicated a song to Terry.

Quickies
Did you know ...
- Terry's run almost came to a sudden and tragic end on the Trans Canada Highway in Cape Breton when a transport truck slammed into a CBC vehicle that was filming him from just a few feet away? The CBC vehicle was knocked right off the road, and the three men in it were injured. If Terry had been a few yards farther ahead he might have been killed.

What were some of the daily problems Terry Fox experienced during his run?

Bad weather could be a problem. If Terry ran close behind his vehicle to get some shelter from strong winds or driving rain, he breathed exhaust fumes. He suffered blisters on his left foot, and blisters and sores where the fitting for his artificial leg rubbed against his stump. In addition to constant exhaustion, he experienced stomach cramps and light-headedness. There were periodic mechanical problems with the artificial leg. Farmers' dogs could be a nuisance. Transport trucks that roared by at high speeds were unnerving and dangerous. In Quebec, some car drivers actually tried to force Terry off the road. (Not until he reached Ontario did Terry have a regular police escort). When Terry stopped for rest breaks or to camp overnight, he often had no privacy. The pressure to attend dinners and receptions after a day's run of 29 miles could be almost overwhelming.

Where did Terry Fox's run end?

Terry had to end his run on September 1 just outside Thunder Bay, Ontario, when it was found that the cancer had spread to his lungs. Running an average of 23.3 miles a day over 143 days, he had covered an astonishing 3,339 miles. By February 1981 his Marathon of Hope had raised $24.17 million for cancer research, realizing Terry's dream of making $1 for each Canadian. Terry died on June 28, 1981, at 4:35 a.m., his favourite time for running.

What is Terry Fox's legacy?

The Terry Fox Marathon of Hope continues to be run in communities across Canada to raise money for cancer research. There are statues of Terry Fox in Ottawa, Thunder Bay, Burnaby, and Victoria. His image has been on a Canadian stamp and the one dollar coin (the only person outside royalty whose image has been on a Canadian coin). Schools, roadways, streets, libraries, sports facilities, a provincial park, a mountain, and a Canadian Coast Guard vessel have been named after him. His story was told in a 1983 HBO TV movie, *The Terry Fox Story*, which starred Eric Fryer and Robert Duval. In 2005, CTV produced another movie, *Terry,* starring Shawn Ashmore. The Nancy Ryan's Singers performed a song called "Run, Terry, Run." Rod Stewart's song "Never Give Up On a Dream" (co-written with Bernie Taupin) was a tribute to Terry Fox, and proceeds from the song go to cancer research.

Further Awards and Honours for Terry Fox

- Companion of the Order of Canada
- Order of the Dogwood (British Columbia's highest civilian award)
- Lou Marsh Trophy of 1980
- Sword of Hope Award from the American Cancer Society, 1980
- Canadian of the year, 1980
- Canadian newsmaker of the year, 1980–81
- Canadian of the decade for 1980s
- TSN Athlete of the Decade for 1980s
- Inducted into the Canadian Sports Hall of Fame
- Placed number 5 in CBC's *Greatest Canadians* program.

What did Steve Fonyo call his cross-Canada run?

Steve Fonyo, born in Montreal on June 29, 1965, lost his left leg to cancer at the age of 12. Inspired by Terry Fox's run, Steve began his Journey for Lives marathon on March 31, 1984, in St. John's, Newfoundland, and completed it on May 29, 1985, in Victoria, British Columbia. He ran 4,923 miles in 424 days at an average of 12 miles per day, and raised $14 million for cancer research. It was an incredible accomplishment, but it was overshadowed by Terry Fox's run of 1980.

Why did Steve Fonyo make the run?

Steve turned 16 the week Terry Fox died. He had looked upon Terry as a true hero, and he wanted to complete the run that Terry had been unable to finish.

How did the public react to Steve Fonyo's run?

At first much of the public reaction was negative. People accused Steve of being a copycat and taking advantage of Terry Fox's popularity. However, as he persevered with his run, the public began to accept what he was doing on its own merits. In 1985, Steve became the youngest person up to that time ever to be made an Officer of the Order of Canada. There are streets named after Steve Fonyo in Kingston, Ontario, and Prince Albert, Saskatchewan, and a beach in Victoria.

How was Rick Hansen inspired to launch his Man in Motion world tour?

Rick Hansen, born in Port Alberni, British Columbia, on August 26, 1957, was an all-star athlete when he lost the use of his legs at age 15 after being thrown from the back of a truck and suffering a spinal injury. Rick's inspiration was his friend Terry Fox's heroic attempt to run across Canada.

What were Rick Hansen's athletic accomplishments before he began his Man in Motion tour?

Rick was the first student with a physical disability to graduate in physical education from the University of British Columbia. He was on teams that won national championships in wheelchair volleyball and basketball. In the 1980 Summer Paralympics he won the gold medal in the 800-metre wheelchair race. He won 19 international wheelchair marathons, including three world championships.

What was the Man in Motion tour?

Rick Hansen's Man in Motion tour was a monumental project to raise money for spinal cord research and to enhance public awareness of the difficulties faced everyday by people with physical handicaps. Simply, Rick decided to manually wheel himself around the world. He started in Vancouver on March 21, 1985. Twenty-six months later, on May 22, 1987, he was back in Vancouver. Rick had covered more than 40,000 miles through 34 countries on four continents, and had raised $26 million. His tour had taken him across North America, Great Britain, Europe, Australia, New Zealand, the Middle East, and the Far East.

What were some of the difficulties Rick Hansen faced?

Rick pushed himself across every sort of terrain and in all kinds of weather. He crossed burning deserts, and navigated ice-covered winter roads. He was slowed down, but not stopped, by floods and gale force winds. The strain of manually propelling his chair day after day resulted in injuries to Rick's shoulders, wrists, and hands. He developed sores from the long hours in his chair. Rick came down with the flu and bladder infections, and had an episode of carbon monoxide poisoning.

Quickies
Did you know ...
- that the song "St. Elmo's Fire" from the soundtrack of the movie of the same name, was written in Rick Hansen's honour by fellow British Columbian David Foster?

How has Canada honoured Rick Hansen?

Rick Hansen was awarded the Lou Marsh Trophy in 1983 (shared with Wayne Gretzky), was made a Companion of the Order of Canada in 1988, and received the Order of British Columbia in 1990. He has been inducted into the Canadian Sports Hall of Fame, Canada's Walk of Fame, and the British Columbia Sports Hall of Fame and Museum where his wheelchair and other items associated with the Man in Motion tour are on display. Several schools and a township have been named after him, and there is a statue of him at General Motors Place in Vancouver.

How many swimming records does Vicki Keith hold?

Vicki Keith of Winnipeg, Manitoba, holds 16 world swimming records and has been the recipient of 41 honours and awards, including the Order of Canada and the Order of Ontario. Her marathon swimming triumphs have all been part of her efforts to raise money for children with physical disabilities. Vicki made her first Lake Ontario crossing in August, 1986. One year later she became the first person to make a double crossing of Lake Ontario. In the summer of 1988 she became the first person to swim across all five Great Lakes: 16 miles across Lake Erie, 47 miles across Lake Huron, 45 miles across Lake Michigan, 20 miles across Lake Superior, and a 24-mile finale across her favourite swimming hole, Lake Ontario.

Who is Josephine Mandamin?

Josephine Mandamin is an Anishinabe grandmother from Thunder Bay, Ontario, whose mission is to draw public attention to the plight of the Great Lakes. Pollution, invasive species, and evaporation due to global warming have the Great Lakes ecosystem on the verge of collapse. Starting in 2003, at the age of 61, Josephine has walked around all five Great Lakes, a total of 10,563 miles. She carries a brass bucket full of lake water, and is usually accompanied by a fellow water walker (friends take turns at this) who carries a pole of eagle feathers. She will complete her mission by walking the length of the St. Lawrence River, from Lake Ontario to the Atlantic Ocean.

Ten Vicki Keith Swimming Accomplishments

- Most crossings (six) of Lake Ontario.
- First butterfly swim across Lake Ontario.
- First butterfly swim across the English Channel.
- Longest solo swim (distance) 58 miles.
- Longest solo swim (time) 63 hours, 40 minutes.
- Continuous swimming (pool) 129 hours, 45 minutes.
- Longest distance, male or female, butterfly, 49 miles.
- Circumnavigation of Sydney, Australia, Harbour (butterfly).
- Crossing of Juan de Fuca Strait, British Columbia.
- Crossing of Catalina Channel, California, (butterfly).

amazing animals

What canine hero was killed on the very day he was chosen to receive a medal for valour?

A German shepherd named King was the mascot of the Canadian drill-boat *John B. King*. In March of 1930, crew member Jack Wylie went through the ice of the St. Lawrence River, and would have drowned if King had not plunged into the frigid water and rescued him. King's bravery was brought to the attention of the Spratt's Dog Hero Award Committee in New York. On June 26, 1930, the committee chose King to receive the award. That very day the *John B. King* was planting dynamite charges in the bed of the St. Lawrence River off Brockville, Ontario, in a channel-widening project. A bolt of lightning struck the ship, detonating the explosives on board and in the riverbed below. The *John B. King* exploded. Only 11 of the 41 men aboard survived. Jack Wylie was among the dead, as was the dog-hero, King.

What part did a horse play in the legend of Simon Girty?

Simon Girty, an American villain but a Loyalist hero, was drinking in a Detroit tavern when American troops came to take possession of the post following the British withdrawal in 1796. If the Americans had captured Girty they probably would have hanged him. But he quickly mounted his horse, and the animal leaped into the Detroit River and swam across to the Canadian side with Girty clinging to its back. Girty later said that when the horse died, he buried it with full military honours.

What is "The Animals' Victoria Cross"?

In 1943, Maria Dickin, founder of a British veterinary charity called the People's Dispensary for Sick Animals (PDSA), instituted the Dickin Medal to honour the accomplishments of animals in war. It is a bronze medallion inscribed with the words FOR GALLANTRY and WE ALSO SERVE. Between 1943 and 1949 it was awarded to 32 pigeons, 18 dogs, three horses, and one cat. The award was revived in 2000.

Four Famous Canadian Horses

- Alfred was General Isaac Brock's horse. This was the horse that carried Brock on his famous ride from Fort George to Queenston on October 13, 1812, to fight an invading American army. Like Brock, Alfred was killed in the battle. There is a monument to Alfred in the village of Queenston.
- Midnight, born in Alberta in 1916, was one of the greatest rodeo horses of all time. Many a rodeo cowboy would boast that he "almost" rode Midnight. Very few actually accomplished it. In 1967, the Midnight Stadium in Fort Macleod was named after the great horse. Midnight was the first animal to be inducted into the Canadian Rodeo Hall of Fame.
- Northern Dancer was Canada's most famous race horse. In 1963, the three-year-old won the Flamingo Stakes, the Florida Derby, the Blue Grass Stakes, the Kentucky Derby, the Preakness Stakes, and the Queen's Plate. He also won the Eclipse Award as the champion three-year-old of 1964. In his two years of racing, Northern Dancer won 14 of his 18 races and never finished worse than 3rd. He then became the most successful sire of the twentieth century. There is a statue of Northern Dancer at Woodbine Racetrack in Toronto.
- Burmese, born in Saskatchewan in 1962, was a product of the RCMP's horse breeding program. At first she was thought to be too small for the Mounties' famous musical ride, but when given the chance, she outperformed all of the other horses and quickly became the star of the show. In 1969, the RCMP gave Burmese to Queen Elizabeth II as a gift. Every year from 1962 to 1986 the queen rode Burmese for the Trooping of the Colour ceremony held in London on her official birthday. Burmese participated in mounted patrols and various pageants, and became one of the most famous horses in England. Burmese died in 1990. In 2005, a bronze statue of Queen Elizabeth mounted on Burmese was unveiled in front of the Saskatchewan Legislative Building in Regina.

What is the Purina Animal Hall of Fame?

Since 1968, the Purina Animal Hall of Fame has been honouring animals that have proven themselves to be pet heroes. As of 2008, the inductees include 114 dogs, 23 cats, and one horse. The Purina Animal Hall of Fame is the featured exhibit at PawsWay in Toronto's Harbourfront Centre.

How did a dog become a Cape Breton hero?

On a summer day in 2000, Corporal Rick Mosher of the Sydney detachment of the RCMP, and his four-year-old Belgian Malinois,

Three Dickin Awards with Canadian Connections

- In 1944, a carrier pigeon named Beach Comber received the Dickin Award for bringing the first news to England of the landing of the Canadian army at Dieppe on August 19, 1942.
- In 2000, a Newfoundland dog named Gander was posthumously honoured with a Dickin Award for gallantry in the Second World War. Gander was the mascot of the Royal Rifles of Canada who were sent to Hong Kong in 1941 to defend the island from the Japanese. During the battle, Gander charged at a group of Japanese soldiers who were threatening some wounded Canadians, and drove them off. Later, when a grenade landed near some Canadian soldiers, Gander picked it up with his teeth and ran with it. The grenade exploded, killing Gander instantly, but the dog had saved the soldiers' lives.
- In 2003, the Dickin Award was given to a German shepherd named Sam for actions in Bosnia-Herzegovina. Sam belonged to the British Royal Army Veterinary Corps, but he was assigned to the Royal Canadian Regiment in Drvar. On April 18, 1998, Sam subdued an armed man who was threatening civilians and military personnel. Six days later, when rioters threatened to attack a compound holding Serbian refugees, Sam held them at bay until reinforcements arrived. Sam's valour undoubtedly saved many lives.

Bandit, were in pursuit of a suspect. On Corporal Mosher's command, Bandit moved in to subdue the suspect. The man slashed at Bandit with a knife that he had concealed in his sleeve. The dog fell back with a severed spinal cord. It then appeared that the suspect was about to attack Corporal Mosher with the knife. Instantly Bandit pounced on the suspect. This time he received a fatal stab wound. But his courageous sacrifice gave Corporal Mosher the precious moments he needed to draw his gun and

Twelve Police Dogs Inducted Into the Purina Animal Hall of Fame

- 1974 — Cloud II; North Bay OPP, Ontario
- 1981 — Lance; Kitchener OPP, Ontario
- 1989 — Dick; Montreal, Sûreté de Québec
- 1992 — Tracker; Sudbury Police, Ontario
- 1993 — Cato; Toronto Police, Ontario
- 1994 — Ewo; Niagara Falls Police, Ontario
- 1997 — Keno; Toronto Police, Ontario
- 2003 — Tracer; N. Vancouver RCMP, British Columbia
- 2004 — Cyr; Saskatoon Police, Saskatchewan
- 2005 — Tim; New Minas RCMP, Nova Scotia
- 2006 — Odin; Calgary Police, Alberta
- 2007 — Ki; Bracebridge OPP, Ontario

apprehend the suspect. In 2001, Bandit was chosen as the recipient of the Ralston Purina Service Dog of the Year Award.

Why was a horse inducted into the Purina Animal Hall of Fame?

In 1978, near Newmarket, Ontario, a Morgan/Quarter Horse named Indian Red drew attention to a helpless elderly woman who had collapsed and fallen into a snow-filled ditch beside a country road on a cold winter night.

How has a dog named Koma saved lives in Afghanistan?

Koma is a female German shepherd trained to sniff out land mines. She can find improvised explosive devices (IEDs) that are otherwise very difficult to detect. Dogs like Koma contribute to the safety of Afghan workers and other civilians, as well as to that of the Canadian military.

Five Cats Inducted Into the Purina Animal Hall of Fame

- 1979 — Tarbot; Caledonia, Nova Scotia: awoke owners and saved them from fire.
- 1984 — Angel; Fredericton, New Brunswick: awoke owners and saved them from fire.
- 1992 — Cali; Toronto, Ontario: alerted sleeping owner of an intruder trying to break into her apartment.
- 2004 — Sosa; Quebec: protected owner from a poisonous snake.
- 2004 — Shadow; Calgary, Alberta: awoke family and saved them from carbon monoxide poisoning.

**question
and feature list**

Courage in Battle

Larger-Than-Life Legends

Valiant Women

Prodigies of Science, Invention, and Medicine

Brave Young Canadians

In the Line of Duty

Civilian Heroes

Intrepid Explorers

Native Icons

Paragons of Politics

Canada's Rebels

Champions of Sport

Martyrs and Marchers

Marathon Men and Women

Amazing Animals

Other Books in the Now You Know Series

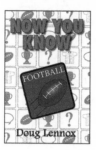

Now You Know Football
978-1-55488-453-7
$19.99

Now You Know Royalty
978-1-55488-415-5
$19.99

**Now You Know
Big Book of Sports**
978-1-55488-454-4
$29.99

**Now You Know
Big Book of Answers 2**
978-1-55002-871-3
$29.99

More Books in the Now You Know Series

Now You Know Soccer 978-1-55488-416-2 $19.99
Now You Know Golf 978-1-55002-870-6 $19.99
Now You Know Hockey 978-1-55002-869-0 $19.99
Now You Know Big Book of Answers 978-1-55002-741-9 $29.99
Now You Know Disasters 978-1-55002-807-2 $9.99
Now You Know Pirates 978-1-55002-806-5 $9.99
Now You Know Extreme Weather 978-1-55002-743-3 $9.99
Now You Know Christmas 978-1-55002-745-7 $9.99
Now You Know Crime Scenes 978-1-55002-774-7 $9.99
Now You Know 978-1-55002-461-6 $19.99
Now You Know More 978-1-55002-530-9 $19.99
Now You Know Almost Everything 978-1-55002-575-0 $19.99
Now You Know Volume 4 978-1-55002-648-1 $19.99

Available at your favourite bookseller.

 DUNDURN PRESS
www.dundurn.com

Did Now You Know satiate your desire for little-known facts, or do you want more? Visit *www.nowyouknow.com*, sign up for the Answer of the Week, and have a little-known fact delivered straight into your inbox!

Printed in the USA
CPSIA information can be obtained
at www.ICGtesting.com
JSHW082206140824
68134JS00014B/465

9 781554 884445